Y0-BRA-544

#10001 OUR BONUS SPECIAL So unique, so unusual, this extraordinary gift captures the entire feeling that we think our gifts should offer! For the first time, we are privileged to offer the only transistorized CB Unit and Hookup—DIRECT WITH GOD!

Once we've installed this unit in your car, boat or mobile home, you can tune in, speak directly on your own private channel to the Deity of your choice. Tell God what you think! Ask God the burning questions you've always wondered about. And all this in privacy.

Pre-selected crystals come with a complete guarantee of 24,000 miles or a lifetime, whichever comes first. But hurry! Don't delay! Order immediately, while our limited supply lasts. Be the first on your freeway to talk with God, DIRECT!

Total CB Unit Cost, including installation and Warranty: $1,111.33.

Additional Crystals: $6.49 each.
License, required by FCC, extra.

#18463 WOMBAT GARDEN DREDGE Powerful 450-foot high-tensile, cable operated dredge removes wombats, moles from underground burrows, simultaneously creates channels for large ornamental lakes, canals. Undamaged wombats and moles can be trained by simple hand-gestures to cultivate remaining garden, plant bulbs (our unique wombat-mole bulb muzzle included). Dredge requires crew of three: captain, first mate, longshoreman, all easily available at local hiring hall (check your waterfront).

Basic Dredge, F.O.B. North Korea, 750 megabucks.
Wombats $350; Moles $22.
Crewmen at prevailing ILA wage, double-time for overtime.

#11212 EJECTA-TRAY No need to struggle to get ice out of a recalcitrant freezer. These trays, powered by silicon batteries, eject cubes at spoken command, propel ice into bucket. (Proper positioning of ice bucket essential.)

Trays, complete with batteries: $17.20 for two. Full dozen $89.50.

#98666 CONTINENTAL DRIFTWARE A completely matched set of tectonic plates. Serves 12.

Total Cost: $99.00 (slightly higher east of California).

#131310 HOME DECLINER FOR THE AGED Dad or Mom need comfort, assistance? Home Decliner lets loved ones sink gently into vat of supportive fluid, complete with simulated TV re-runs, Geritol, decreasing nonsexual massage. Vat freezes at moment of Actual Death, leaves large, translucent conversation piece.

F.O.B. Los Angeles: $7,500.00.

#05055 STAPLER (Live) Our exclusive "Praying Mantis Stapler" literally pounces on your documents and grips them firmly between front claws! And, when work day is over for you, Mantis is still busy, devouring mosquitoes and small insects—just the thing for keeping the entire office clean as a pin!

Mantis (complete with plastic pouch of 2 insects) for starter $3.98. Green only.

#00098 BONSAI MIDGET-MAGIC
For everything there is a season and a time, so why not keep everything just at its peak moment of perfection? With our BONSAI MIDGET-MAGIC, shape your environment to your needs as you quickly wind-and-bind trees, bushes, even small children to create instant art. Method proved completely satisfactory by centuries of Oriental women. Comes complete with wind-and-bind bondage strips, weatherproof aluminum stakes and illustrated, easy-to-follow, step-by-step stunting (dwarfing) instructions. Only **$49.95.** (Owner must supply own living specimens; these are not included in package!)

Imported From Canton

#87964 ACTIVATED SLUDGE
No, it's not a pretty name, but burglars and other intruders aren't pretty either.* PROTECT YOURSELF: the moment our Sludge senses an intruder in your home, it will leap from its retaining pot, track down the intruder and cloak him in suffocating blanket of slime. Watch as he writhes helplessly, is carried away by municipal sanitation officers. Sludge returns to pot on coded command from owner. Feeds on left-overs, economical to maintain.

Per gallon: $250.

* Recent USDA studies indicate that burglars and other intruders are 72.7% less pretty than the rest of us.

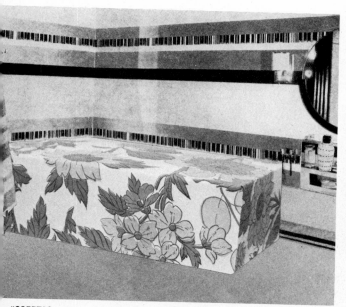

#2255789 ALL PURPOSE, PURE VINYL DECORATED TUB COVERS
Company pop in unexpectedly and catch you with a filthy bathtub? Never—not when you can throw this over the top of your tub. Just set up the four aluminum struts and fling your cleverly decorated cover into place, and there you have it: extra seating and a completely neat bathroom! Delight family and friends alike with the clever sayings and assorted motifs decorating this cover. Any bathroom, from modern to Victorian, dresses up in just seconds for only **$66.00** per cover. This includes shipping, four aluminum struts and simulated gold link chain frame.

#05991 CAPTAIN HOOK POTHOLDERS
Magnetic potholders attach instantly to any size claw, aluminum or stainless steel. Also available in smaller model for stainless steel dentures.

Assorted motifs and colors, only $2.98 each.

Caution: Do not use near television sets, as magnetic field reverses pictures.

#16894 HOME VOMITORIUM Why deprive yourself of goodies you really want? Do as Romans did, with our exclusive HOME VOMITORIUM. Cabinet only six feet square, has all attachments for plumbing, chrome feather-holder. Choose from knotty pine, Mediterranean oak, Art Deco.

Unassembled: $1,750.00. You pay only for local installation.

First 500 buyers receive ABSOLUTELY FREE a case of resinated wine!

#9540 JOAN OF ARC BARBECUE LIGHTER Ignites by simple prayer. Works with any size barbecue unit, from smallest Hibachi to giant fire pit. Bonus offer includes bundle of faggots (14) of finest Georgia fatwood to get blaze going instantly.

Total Cost, including one bundle of faggots: $12.47. Shipping included.

Imported from Rome, GA.

#131305 MUMMY CORPSE CANDLES From the catacombs of Rome, this special treat for discriminating party givers. Mummies, impregnated with bitumen, will burn for 6 to 8 hours, depending on height.

Per foot, $75.00; sure-fire igniter included. Tested by leading basilicas.

#131303 PERSONALIZED EYE-COINS When it comes time to place coins on the eyes of your dead, will you have the right coins available? Think ahead! Coins (available only in pairs) can be supplied with loved one's favorite photograph or saying. Have vacuum base, cannot slip, cause embarrassment. From Charon Corporation, the only suppliers.

$75.00 and up.

Unnatural Acts & Conclusions

#010203 **UNNATURAL ACTS AND CONCLUSIONS** At the end of your tether? Unable to see a way out? Don't despair! Just follow the simple guidebook our experts have assembled and with just one unnatural act, we guarantee you'll reach total satisfaction. For the novice, it's a virtual encyclopedia of information, and for those whose needs have been unsatisfied with even extremist delights, the supplement (included at no extra cost) will take you one step beyond to the most bizarre unnatural conclusions imaginable.

Please specify area of desired experience:
   a. Sexual
   b. Religious
   c. Los Angeles
   d. Other

If other, please explain.

Waiver must be signed before we can send this exciting gift to you or the loved one of your choice. Clip and Send:

   I am Over 21 years old ___ and qualify as an adult for this gift.
   I am Under 21 years old ___ and qualify as an adult for this gift.
   I am Other ___ and qualify as an other for this gift.

(Cost available upon request and completion of above information.)

#56 MATCHED BLUE WHALES We can only offer this one pair—the Ultimate Gift—to the first lucky buyer. Our Matched Blue Whales, Ed and Marjorie, have been specially trained by our resident whale-trainer, Gepetto, who assures us they are tame enough to hand feed. As an additional bonus to the lucky owner, we include a unit that attaches easily (complete instructions included) on the back of Ed and Marjorie to provide AM and FM reception within the 200 mile limit. Easily wired for stereo at small additional cost.

Total package: $5,000.00 (Includes one month plankton supply. Additional refills extra).

#02 THE GASTRO/ NOMEAT This multi-purpose kitchen chainsaw, lathe, dark room and log roller makes a meal in minutes as it slices, buffs, sands and grinds your vegetables to a patina you never thought possible. Then it develops an entire meal while rolling papers for your barbecue. No kitchen can be called complete without this item at the cook's disposal.

Total Cost: $400.22 or $14.99 for a limited time only with attached coupon.

#666 JOHN THE BAPTIST SILVER PLATE Well-known Middle Eastern firm, Salome Industries, has hammered this presentation plate, no two alike, in their own cisterns. Talk about a head trip! Please specify neck size: 14½-17½. Available only with very short sleeves. **Standard: $22.50. Draggled in mud and despised: $77.00.**

#97276 BLIVETS From stockings to French Jeans, there's nothing that our "Blivet" can't stuff! Reduces feet an entire size and can take a normal size 14 (American) and place into French Jean size 26 without more than a moment's discomfort. Also useful for stuffing sofa cushions, sausages (Italian) and sausages (German.)

Blivet, complete with attachments, $29.95.

F.O.B. Rome

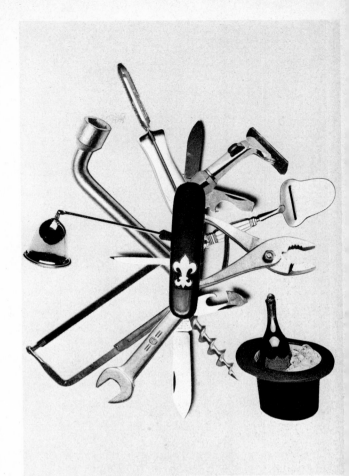

#6091300-P FRENCH UNDERGROUND ARMY KNIFE Seventy-two different functions in one compact pocket model—THE KNIFE, of finest French underground steel. Unfold it bit by bit: it's a hacksaw, a double-edged hatchet, a portable wireless, even a lavatory, all in an instant!

Flick the appropriate blade, and voila! You have a vegetable scraper and pineapple corer. Plus all the standard features you expect in such a knife: scissors, nail file and escargot extractor. Our newest model features a complete set of tools for wilderness survival: car jack, socket wrenches and lug nut remover. What more can we say? It's all here in one clever, compact model, featuring elegant, versatile chrome and black enamel finish.

Total cost: $29.95, includes 72 multi-purpose functions and accessories. Shipping weight: 45 lbs.

#404040404 HOME DEGENERATOR Works on AC/DC current. Swings! Never a power loss! When the party gets going, this keeps it going; just plug it in, and watch it snap into action. Completely degenerates, refreshes any room in seconds.

Total Cost: $49.95.

F.O.B. New Jersey

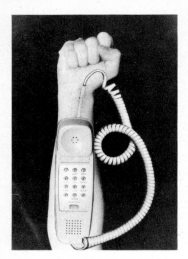

#139002   EXTRUDE-A-PHONE

Never a telephone handy at the right moment? Extrude-A-Phone begins with tiny capsule painlessly implanted in hand or upper arm, uses electrical resources of YOUR OWN VENOUS SYSTEM to contact nearest substation. Less than three weeks of growth, training and Princess touch-tone phone will emerge from your skin at will, re-enter as soon as vital call is completed. No discomfort, no awkwardness, no need for remote call-back systems.

Flesh color (specify Caucausian, Black, Chicano).

Note: Initial implantation may require fee from local telephone company; no charge for extensions.

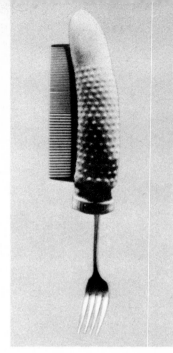

#477477   ENDLESS SUMMER BEACH BRA

Truly unusual, hot-colored Beach Bra comes with AS MANY CUPS AS WEARER PERSONALLY REQUIRES, minimum of one to maximum of eight! What a conversation piece for Miami or Waikiki vacation!

PLEASE: Carefully specify *number* of cups, *size* of each individual cup, *arrangement* (left, right; horizontal, vertical rows). If arrangement very unlikely, please enclose paper pattern.

Priced at only $29.95 per cup; if two or more Beach Bras ordered, $24.95 per cup (multiply cup price by *total* number of cups ordered).

Each garment made to *your individual order*, so please allow 6-8 weeks for fabrication, delivery. Sweet accompanying FREE GIFT: cassette or eight-track recording of up-tempo "Third Nipple Theme." Specify cassette or 8-track, hard rock or disco version.

#7979   COMBINATION COMB, FORK AND VIBRATOR. This is the ultimate multipurpose tool.

Total Price: $21.50 plus removable batteries.

#71296   GLINDA THE GOOD PUNCH-AND- GROW CYCLAMATE GARDEN

Dieters, diabetics, grow Mother Nature's organic saccharins and cyclamates on sunny kitchen window sills. Punch the tiny pot (punching glove included) and watch it begin to produce. Saccharins form crystalline powder, cyclamates produce graduated pills, larger as summer sun intensifies. Free entire family from the Tyranny of Refined Sugar!

Six Saccharin Starters, only $7.50. Full Dozen: $13.00. Cyclamates only in Sets of Four: $6.39.

FDA Application Pending

#DC-10 DINING ACCESSORIES
Love SERIOUS dinner parties? Our black-and-white dinner plates are for you and your guests, who will appreciate the stunningly etched scenes from Goya's THE THIRD OF MAY, 1808. Executions, blood perfectly reproduced. **Set of twelve $114.00.**

Accompanying salad plates show mutilations from Goya's THE BODIES OF BREBENT AND LALLEMANT MUTILATED BY THE IROQUOIS. **Entire set: $69.95.**

SOON TO COME: Sterling Silver Inquisition place settings, flatware, Condemnation pattern.

#32 LA ROCHEFOUCAULD MAXIM GUN
Don't worry again about sudden terrible silences at your cocktail parties. Just touch the firing stud and this inobtrusive weapon (can be disguised as vase) projects clever maxim or epigram to get conversation really moving. Turn stud to the left and maxim bursts in mid-air; to the right, fine-focus on undesirable guest.

Rapid-moving belt cartridge contains 500 maxims, no two alike.

From Mozambique, $495.
Replacement cartridges, $49.95.

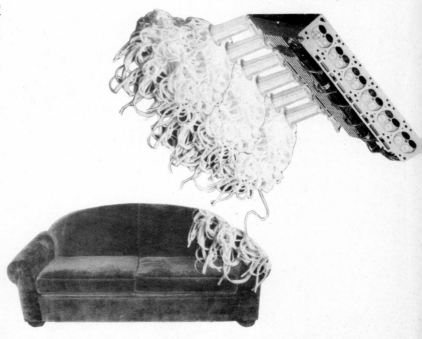

#4897 CROCHET A SOFA
Slipcovers are now a thing of the past! Crochet an entire new sofa in just three or less spare evenings. Just place your fingers into unique five finger crochet blow gun at appropriately marked indentions, direct the yarn (included) and exhale. Light as air, yarn responds instantly. Even a beginner can crochet two cushions plus a whole back of a sofa in three hours. Just send us the size of the sofa plus desired color: Bliss Blue (a deep, rich, sea-blue), Morning Thunder (an elegant bluish mauve), Terra Clay (apricot-brown), and Enveloping Black. Write for complete list. Instructions included.

Total Cost: $42.99 plus yarn.

#980667 CLONE-A-PHONE
All you need is any part of an old telephone; borrow a friend's receiver, cord, even an old dial, and with our kit at your command, CLONE YOUR OWN PHONE! Watch as your instrument takes shape in its own Petri Culture Dish; day by day it will develop all needed vital elements and within two weeks, a complete system is yours: telephone, poles, even extensions! And a modest additional charge gets you our Giant Culture-And-Incubate Bottle that will clone an entire repairperson for you (necessary fingernail peelings not included).

Imagine the money you'll save in just one year!

Total Cost: $667,900.13 Includes Petri Dish for Clone-A-Phone. $55.26 Additional charge for Giant Bottle.

A CANAL FOR ALL SEASONS

Whatever your size requirements, we have the canal to fill the bill! From largest to smallest, each completely ready to go.

#9786   THE PANAMA CANAL   The very largest one we offer: locks in perfect condition, three used Senators and a dictator of our choice. Only one of these available: order early to assure yourself of this gem. We include insect repellent at no extra cost!

Price: $990,000.21 (Please send cashier's check).

#9787   THE ALIMENTARY CANAL   Useful in more constricted environments, this canal also features lox in perfect condition. Comes complete with easy installation instructions.

Yours for only $44.25 (Cash, check or money order accepted).

#9788   THE ROOT CANAL   For those with limited space, or apartment dwellers. Fully portable.

Price: $234.56 (Includes gold cap, when available

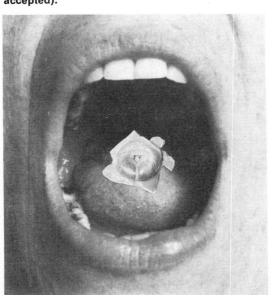

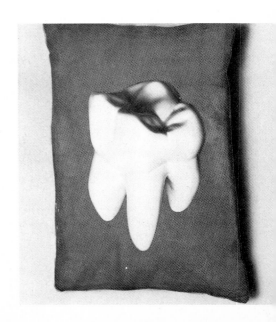

#84722 BICENTENNIAL TUBA Only a few of these magnificent instruments remain from the Nation's Birthday! Tuba stands eight feet tall, on intricately carved applewood stand: depicts *Washington* at Valley Forge, crossing Delaware, swearing Presidential Oath, authentic death mask.
Battery powered (12 volt heavy truck battery), Tuba plays Souza marches, presents genuine fireworks display (Des Moines, Iowa, 1906), finally emits phosphorescent replica of Francis Scott Key that glows in darkness for hours!

Shipped from Fort Sumter: $1,665.00 complete.

#4222 BLACK FOREST CLOCK Created by the intricate woodcarvers of the Black Forest, this one-foot high, wood-grained plastic clock features a radium dial, for easy-to-read-in-any-light numbers. When the tiny bird announces the hour, Ben and Karbie slide out of their quaint house and pose effectively for a full minute. Midnight and High Noon feature both dolls in an assortment of random positions. Magnifying glass included at no extra cost.

Total Assembled Price: 1500 Swiss Francs

Made in Germany
Assembled in England

#38664838 THE SAVAGE BLENDER For adventurous cooks, anyone into the new African cuisine. THE SAVAGE BLENDER. Two gutta-percha bowls, set of six honed steel machetes, three natives (large, medium, demi). Relax in your kitchen, let our equipment do it for you!

**$1,750.00, plus three steerage-class berths from Lagos. Oral Cookbook Included.
THERE IS NO WARRANTY ON THIS ITEM.**

#8880 MUSICAL SURFBOARD Ride the waves or sit on the beach and strum away! Your Musical Surfboard is completely water resistant and folds up to travel anywhere you do: from Hilo to Molokai. Economy model: **$165.00** Optional slide guitar attachment at slight extra cost. Or: order the complete unit for only **$170.99** and we'll throw in Don Ho's Greatest Hawaiian Guitar Hits—free! Easy to assemble; comes with own cardboard carrying case in Banyan Finish. Two colors to choose from: Pipeline Pink, or Roller Red.

#598633 THE QUASIMODO SELF-TIMING FONDUE SET We had a hunch no other Fondue Set could compete with ours, and you'll agree it's the finest of its kind. For home or commercial purposes, it's quick, easy and self-contained. Unit has pendulum type stir mechanism to keep fat hot, cheese lump-free; when it's ready to go, bell rings to let you know it's time to dip and cook. Adjusts to any height in an instant.

Total Cost: $29.95 plus tax and small shipping surcharge. Imported From France

#59682 GIANT BIRD FEEDER Just before the major automobile company that designed these modern high impact tubes went out of business, we bought the entire remaining stock: 5,000 of these 20-foot beauties, then we drilled openings at 4-foot intervals. Now we offer them to bird lovers who have always wished they could feed the Giant Birds, but until now had no way to attract Golden Eagles, California Condors and Large Albatrosses. Just fill up your Giant Bird Feeder with our special formula feed (3 parts seed to 2 parts dessicated fish bone) and watch those rare birds flock to your feeder from miles away! Isn't it assuring to know you can help keep one of the endangered species alive? (Caution: feeder should be placed at least 40 feet from house.)

Total Cost: $49.95 (Includes shipping and sample bag of bird feed).

#6875 OUR HOME DECORATOR The clever homemaker's dream: easy-instruction kit tells proper way to lacquer pizza and make other fashion-wise home accessories! A complete section is devoted to the faking of Irish artifacts, and, for the more advanced student, "How to Weave Your Own Scotch." Includes the hows-and-whys of Bagpipe Cementing, the proper placement of empty scotch bottles for seating arrangements at a Scotch Party. Plus: A complete history of Haggis, and one petrified sample, included at no extra cost.

Total Kit: $76.23.

#4221 UNDIGITAL CLOCK *Full features* such as standard flip back numbers, showing hour, day of the week, month and year, and also coming cataclysms! Just specify area in which clock is to be used, and you will have advance warnings of tsunami, tornadoes even earthquakes. Early warning chimes out delicately every fifteen seconds, then turns to shrill alarm (stays on until cataclysm is over or electricity fails). You won't sleep through the next disaster with this warning system! Works on any household current.

Comes in Decorator colors: Al Dente Ivory, Pesto Green, Suede Blue and Marinara Red, at the unbelievably low price of only **$199.95** (each) with an unconditional guarantee for owner's lifetime or lifetime of clock.

Made in Italy

#01119 MAGNETIC SADDLE For the beginning rider, this is a must! Magnetic saddle keeps you firmly affixed: you'll never fall off, will feel you were born to the saddle and have lead in your pants. Actually, it isn't lead, but a cunningly designed riding habit which features magnets in each of the pockets and along the thighs. This complete unit comes in your size and your choice of English or Western.

Riding pants, crop, saddle: **Total Cost: $550.00** (Horse not included.)

When ordering, please send body measurements and size of horse.

#74936 VOICE-OPERATED DOORMAT Plush doormat, available in wide range of colors, asks "Friend or Foe" when stepped on. If password is not quickly given, electrocutes unwanted visitor.

Price: $775.00.

#45612 CUSTOMIZED KITCHEN Don't be ashamed of your old-fashioned kitchen—Remodel! In four or less hours, turn a dingy, shabby kitchen into a modern looking, shining tract model.

It's all done with our custom fit-and-spray illuminated kitchen panel kits. Just start at one corner, then stretch and bend each unit around existing fixtures. In minutes, you transform an old-fashioned stove into a mock micro-wave! Simply send specifications (include blueprints of existing floor plans, size of counters, appliances desired); choose from imitation Formica, or elegant simulated marble wallboard. All cooking-unit fronts are Contact mylar; a snap to put on. Dials included.

Total Package: $99.95 and up.

BEFORE

BEFORE

AFTER

#777   VLAD-THE-IMPALER SKEWERS Exquisite European craftsmanship, these skewers adjust to fit every need, from individual portions to entire goat or side of beef, when fully extended. Stress-tested for up to 250 lbs., versatile skewers are useful with Home Rotisserie or Restaurant service. Porcelain enameled hand grips have floral motifs, and each set of six is made of finest metal finished in hardwood. Our low price of **$22.95** delivers these to your door, and you'll want to order at least two sets: one for you and one for that special someone.

Imported from Transylvania

(Caution: These are not recommended as fencing equipment, since standard foil tips do not fit the points.)

YOUR FAVORITE MOMENTS, CAPTURED IN BRONZE

#4333   THE SUNDAY *NEW YORK TIMES*. Have your favorite news edition immortalized by our new bronze-a-bit method which insures every page, including want ads, will remain just as you read it that day, preserved in wondrous bronze. Stand included.

Total Price: $56.66 plus shipping and handling charges of $7,987.00.

#4333-A   THE *WASHINGTON POST*. Same as above, but with addition of recording alleged to be actual cough of "Deep Throat."

Total Price: $.79 (mono) $3.98 (stereo)

#5   BRONZE LEG CAST To remember what the final downhill run was all about, we will preserve it in bronze. If both legs were broken, we will be glad to place both on suitable stands to use as bookends or large ashtrays.

Total Price: $762.00 per cast, including stand. Please send cast or casts after surgical removal has been completed. Not covered under Medicare.

#12509   ANTIQUE TUMBRILS Our exclusive English import, each of these solid oak carts guaranteed to have taken convicted murderers to London gallows, 17th, 18th century. No two alike, some authentically blood-stained. Use as cocktail tables, exciting base for summer barbecue.

$1,500.00 and up, depending on murderer.

Biography of murderer included, no extra charge.

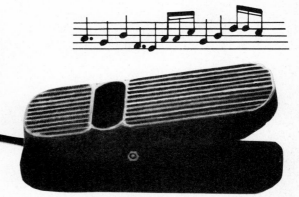

#34458   C.P.E. BACH PORTABLE FOOT PEDAL Talk about Sing Along With Mitch! Portable Foot Pedal allows you to accompany performances of *St. John Passion*, Handel's *Messiah*, Berlioz *Requiem*. Just pump: foot pedal does the rest, translates full vocal score into sole of your foot (remove shoe before using). Quadraphonic model available, requires well-adjusted couple; tested on Siamese twins. Specify foot size, voice (as, 7AA Coloratura).

Prices vary, inquire.   **Shipped from Bayreuth**

#098760 POTTING SHED
Who wouldn't be proud to
show off a potting shed as
special as THIS ONE? Choose
from thousand-year-old
Sequoia Gigantea or the
equally elegant Heart of Red
wood and turn your potting
shed into sanctuary setting
where small plants flourish
and grow. Only a few of these
pre-fab units are left, so
hurry! When these are gone,
we'll probably be unable to
repeat this extraordinary
offer.

Total cost: $900.00
(Please specify species of
endangered lumber
desired.)

#25522 HISTORIC GIRL SCOUT COOKIES

It's taken years to gather this remarkable collection: every Girl Scout Cookie sold in the United States since they were first introduced! Last full set sold made record price at Sotheby's.

Each cookie preserved in argon, then surrounded with permanent plastic shell, mounted on genuine walnut plaque. Your full name or monogram included.

Entire Set (30 Cookies): $7,750.00. Can Be Financed.

#131306 PLAID YOURSELF Feel fish-belly white and out of it on the beach this summer? Cover your whole lovely body with our clan tartans, available in Royal Stuart, Black Watch, Queen Victoria Balmoral, others. Spray can reproduces pattern perfectly. Comes with delightful bagpipe pendant. Haggis optional.

**16-oz. Spray Can: $11.50.
Vat: $255.00.**

Lady Macbeth Bath Oil

#15511551 LADY MACBETH BATH OIL Treat yourself like royalty! All the perfumes of Arabia leave your body soft and supple, soothed and refreshed. Afterward, the cunning container can be used for all sorts of purposes; knife holder or jewel-box.

All this for only: $2.98.

Imported from Glasgow

#4789 OUR SHOWER SUIT For those moments when you want to wash your hair without getting your clothing completely soaked, just slip on our Shower Suit, zip up, and wash away! Clean hair in minutes, and the rest of you remains TOTALLY dry and ready to go.

All seams are high impact plastic, and this triple gauge vinyl inflates in seconds, lasts for years.

Only $12.97 plus shipping: one size fits all.
(Head gear and bicycle pump slight additional cost. Packed in matching Vinyl Briefcase: add $22.00)

#099870 MARAT BATH SET An exciting concept for home bathers. From the C. Corday firm, this matching bath set is so sensual, so exotic, you'll want one for every bathroom in your house. Comes in the newest shade: Le Sang Rouge.

Total Cost: $24.98

Imported From France

#90755 PHOENIX MOBILE Legendary Phoenix, symbol of survival. Now *three* lovely phoenixes in beautiful mobile; dramatic as light strikes wings, claws, dorsal feathers. Twice yearly, mobile ignites, flares, reduces surrounding to ash, then coaleses to small porcelain eggs. Refrigerate: IN ONE MONTH, entire mobile re creates itself. Best statement of survival you can imagine. Shipped in asbestos envelope, ready to hang.

Total Cost: $15.99 per mobile.

(Note: Check homeowner's policy for exclusion items: if phoenix is not *specifically* stated, you are completely insured.)

#339960 FUNNY WHEN YOU'RE SICK Trained staff of hospital clowns, dress strangely, eat your grapes, jeer at you, sit on bed in order to induce varicose veins.

$17.50 Per Hour.
Must have waiver from patient.

GIFTS FOR YOUR FAVORITE PHYSICIAN

#5522 CHESS SET For the doctor, it's LIVER TO SPLEENSPAWN TWO! Our elaborate, hand-crafted chess set features the organs of the human body in living color. Leisure hours are never wasted with this gift, as checking and mating are really learning and playing, all in one. What better measure of your thoughtfulness than this magnificent present!

Total Cost: $22.95 (includes board and instructions).

#5532 STEREO-STETHOSCOPE Our Stereo-Stethoscope, for the young doctor or intern who just doesn't have the time to enjoy music, but wants to know what's going on. Imagine: even the busiest intern can work and play to acid rock and never miss a beat. Fully

transistorized and authentic to the last detail, the dials are cunningly concealed in the earpieces. No one will ever guess!

Total Cost: $15.66
Made In Japan

#3457 THE HOME DEFIBRILLATOR It took our engineers months to reduce that bulky hospital defibrillator to a portable model, making it available for instant home use. Fully transistorized, it delivers a 7,000 volt jolt to the faint of heart. Paddles included, plus complete instructions. Just plug in, stand back, and zap away! Also useful as a complete hair depilator.

Total Cost: $5,000.00 (includes rechargable batteries)
A.M.A. Approval Pending (as always)

#5522

#5532

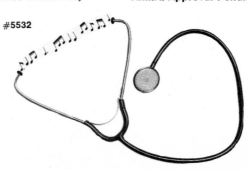

#3457

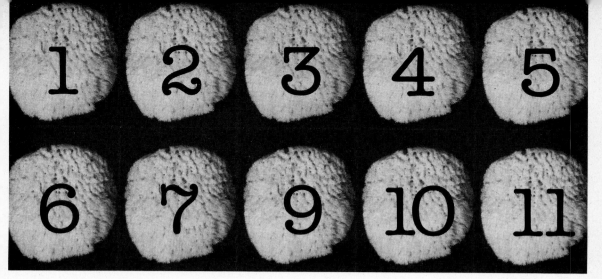

#438576 SURGICAL SPONGES   If you plan any abdominal operation at home, you need our sterilized surgical sponges; each sponge numbered, so it's easy to make an accurate count.

Dozen: $22.50
Gross: $250.00 (for lengthy or repeated operations)

Keep for 6 months in home freezer.

#3 NEW LUNGS FOR SMOKERS   We all know someone we love who needs at least one of these. And for those smokers, we offer three complete models of our famous Lung. Our plain, or Iron model, features a full complement of lobes (superior, middle, inferior) and is packed in its own sterile serous membrane (pleura) for quick insertion and removal.

Our elegant Barcelona model, the filter tip, features a cork pluera and a hand respirator the smoker can carry with him.

Or if that someone is really special to you, you'll want the deluxe model, our Franco version. Entooled in gilt Spanish Leather with intricate detailings highlighting the inferior lobe and packaged in olive oil.

Please specify which:
Iron: $25,000.00 F.O.B. Boston Memorial Hospital.
Barcelona: $35,000.00 F.O.B. Houston.
Franco: $50,000.00 F.O.B. Salamanca.

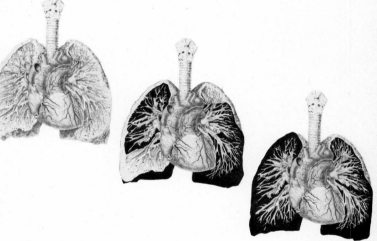

#00000-0   RICHARD NIXON DEATH MASK   Mask modeled from former President's features, as discarded in Washington, D.C., San Clemente, elsewhere. Mask extremely flexible, will be useful on any occasion. Needs occasional lubrication to prevent flaking.

$2.50 includes shipping, crating.

#1848   THE CHARLES BOVARY ORTHOPEDIC BOOT
One size fits all.

Total Cost: 59.95.

#9991 LOTS FOR LESS Owning land is like having money in the bank: it keeps on growing! You choose which of these three special gifts (only one per person available) you'd like and we'll send you a sample of your purchase to show friends and neighbors. Better than photographs, your holdings are displayed, right there, on your coffee table!

Lot 9991-A PRINCE EDWARD ISLAND. Perfect for hunting and fishing. Suitable for entire family and other relatives.

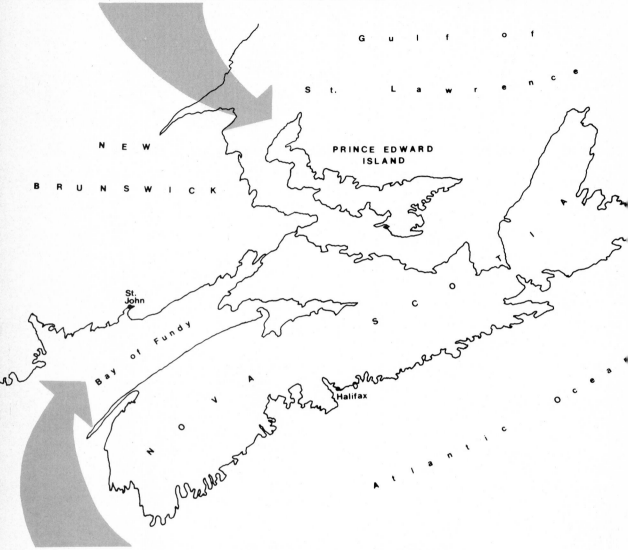

Lot 9991-B BAY OF FUNDY. (Tides extra) The most novel piece of real estate ever offered.

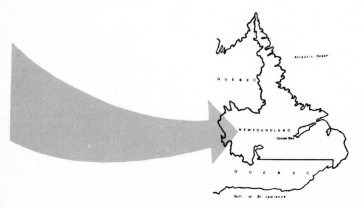

Lot 9991-C NEWFOUNDLAND.
For those who prefer a cooler climate. We also include a smoked salmon with this gift package.

Write for price list and complete details.

#400 AUTOCLAVE This completely sterile harp is the perfect gift for the invalid confined to bed. Nonallergenic, pollen-free, surgical banlon strings are pre-tightened and need no tuning. Accompanying booklet with 15 easy tunes, Bach to Stravinsky, included with fingering.

Autoclave plus booklet for only $500.99. Shipping extra.

#2020 HEARING FORK Ashamed of being deaf? No longer will you have to miss important parts of any conversation. Just place this fork in your mouth and sounds are instantly transmitted via tines to eardrum. For the hearing impaired, a gift that shows you really care!

Total Cost: $12.99 per fork.

Caution: Do *not* use this item for anything other than its intended purpose and keep out of the reach of small children.

#09800 OEDIPUS COMPACT CONTACT LENSES Just send us your prescription and we'll see to all your needs! Lenses of high density polystyrene can be used for any number of purposes when not needed for immediate vision. Each is a perfect pearl holder and strong enough to core apples.

Comes in attractive carrying case. Sanitary, nonporous material is virtually indestructible.

Only $49.95 a pair; half the price of any other custom lenses.

Please allow three weeks for expert grinding and delivery.

Imported From Greece

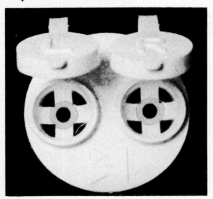 

Side View

#2671 THE SCHLAFLY REPLACEABLE HYSTERECTOMY For women who believe biology is destiny, and who due to circumstances feel unable to fulfill their basic function in life, this surgically sterile kit comes with a complete ovaric-uterine transplant.

In three delicious flavors: Chocolate, Strawberry or Cream of Tartar. Please specify choice and item will be shipped in plain brown wrapper.

Total Cost: $4,562.11, includes one week's post-operative consultation. (Spumoni-flavor available at slight additional cost.)

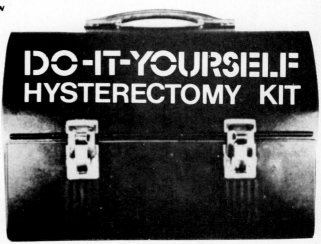

#1111111 HERALDIC BANDAGES, MEDICATIONS! What can say more about the elegance of your household than your own family crest lovingly embossed on our remarkable range of pre-cut, self-applying bandages, surgical strappings, casts, genuine aged hickory-wood crutches, common household medications? If you don't have an authenticated family crest, let us create one for you. Send surname, mother's maiden name (if mother a maiden), favorite sport, television serial, disease. Crests surgically sterile.

From Molokai, sold only as full kit: $59.95.

Note: For embossing prescription medicine, consent of family physician is required.

#0000-11 HOME ANESTHESIA Render self, friends and companions senseless in only seconds with this simple-to-operate, complete kit. Attaches to blower unit of furnace.

Total Cost: $9.99.

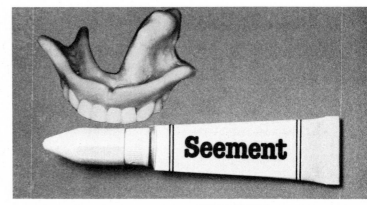

#125698 CEMENT A REAL CONVERSATION PIECE! Temporary cement for cleft palates; avoids expensive operations. Colors: sputum, phlegm, mucus.

Ten-Ounce Squeeze-Tube: $10.50.   Set Of Three: $25.00.
Bulgarian Import

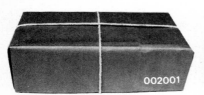
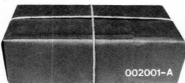
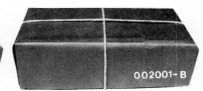

ORGAN TRANSPLANTS

#002001 Inexpensive Magnetic Card Typewriter can be tied to many household appliances: dishwasher, garbage disposal, and electronic organ. Then, sit back and type musical scale: all appliances respond simultaneously. Included: program for Bach *B Minor Mass*; many other available at extra charge. Typewriter must be purchased separately, after that, you're on your own with our heavy-duty connecting cords.

Mass: $27.98; Other masses at discount.

#002001-A Bored, dissatisfied, feel you should have been somebody else, mother really wanted son/daughter? Problem's easily solved. Inexpensive change is only cosmetic, can be reversed: includes appropriate body hair, features, organs (specify male, female, other), behavioral manual.

Special One-Time Price: $32.50.

#002001-B PERMANENT CHANGE From our hidden laboratories at Marrakesh! Easy-to-follow anatomical charts, full color illustrations, 100-Blade Swiss Army Scalpel Set, bandages, sutures included. Comes with ABSOLUTELY FREE 24-hour anesthesia packet. Again, specify sex changing from, sex changing to, if known. If not known, send drawing. Ask about our new experimental programs: we can transform you into animals or plants. Special charges for marsupials, tubers. Write for complete price list, free estimate.

HOME ENVIRONMENTS

#65 THE TITANIC We can't guarantee against water damage, but if your house is structurally sound, we can provide you with this exciting new home environment. Comes complete with iceberg, towed to nearest port of entry, and choir rendition of "Nearer My God, To Thee," plus our assurance of unsinkable pleasure.

Total Cost: $6,809.00 including iceberg.
West of Mississippi, please add $6.00 extra shipping charge.
Examination of structural integrity, $411.00 extra.

#64 THE HINDENBERG Assemble this kit in one corner of your living room, or have our technicians assemble it for you, then enjoy the complete Hindenberg atmosphere. Included with your purchase: one fire extinguisher, a full supply of hydrogen, plus a stereo recording of announcer retching.

Total Cost: $54.95 (for do-it-yourself kit) or $54.95 (with our technicians assisting) Victims excluded.

#980 THE STORMING OF BUNKER HILL Let our skilled technicians build for you, in one corner of your house, a complete replica of this famous battle. Includes one (1) treadmill, fourteen (14) matched muskets, and complete assortment of tattered New England clothing, plus flag. Recording of "Don't fire until you see the whites of their eyes!" also included at no additional cost.

Total Package: $10,000.00

#980-A THE STORMING OF BUNKER HILL For Anglophiles, this package is similar to one described above, except treadmill (1) built going downhill. Includes matching red coats (new; please specify size), polished virgin muskets and recording of "This is no way to fight a war. Don't you people know the rules?" in cockney accent.

Total Cost: £7,359 6p.

#131312   ASSORTED HOOVES Spike heels are out, platforms are out, what next? Newest Paris fashion says hooves; we have in sets of two or four, depending on your species. Specify centaur, satyr, cloven.

All Hooves $35.00 for Two—Simply multiply for number of additional limbs.

Grown in our own laboratories.

#00709   BI-SEXUAL THERMOMETER
For those occasions when pink or blue is not appropriate, our bi-sexual thermometer takes the worry out of being close.
   A perfect gift for the baby shower, those undergoing sex change operations and any hip household!

Only $2.99, attractively gift boxed in chrome.

#54321   MUSEUM REPLICA GLANDS
Pituitary, thyroid, pancreas, enlarged baroque liver: each taken from suffering donor, carefully mounted, glazed, and then made part of a unique conversation piece in rubber tubing and silver wire. Glands carefully selected to show signs of fatty deterioration: these patterns of marbling are never seen except in cases of extreme disease.

Sold by weight, at $350.00 per troy ounce; largest baroque liver, a true collector's item, weighs seventeen pounds.

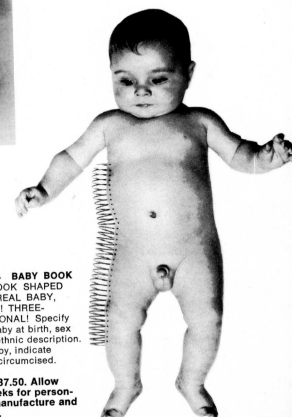

#4837264   BABY BOOK
BABY BOOK SHAPED LIKE A REAL BABY, LIFELIKE! THREE-DIMENSIONAL! Specify size of baby at birth, sex (if any), ethnic description. If boy baby, indicate whether circumcised.

Price: $37.50. Allow four weeks for personalized manufacture and delivery.

#0008 DNA RECOMBINANT KIT For the home scientist, the *only* authorized kit that allows total freedom to manipulate genetic strains. Experiment in the privacy of your own laboratory or kitchen with the genetic heritage of the planet on which you live. Alter, recombine exciting variations, as you discover and produce new life forms, bacterial strains, viral infusions, with no limit except your own imagination!

A set of easy-to-assemble Double-Helixes is included with your kit to get you started. After that, the sky's the limit!

**Total Cost: $66.99 plus shipping.
Masks and Isolation Chamber not included.**

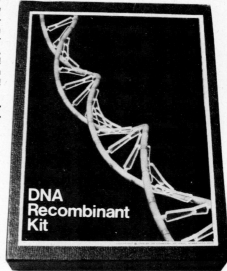

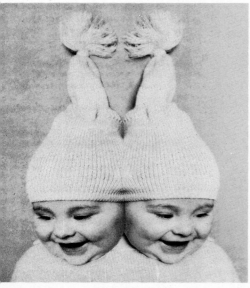

#222222222 SIAMESE TWIN CAP(S) One size fits two. In washable stretch fabric. Colors: blue, pink, or half and half.

Total Cost: $3.99.

#77 SEEING EYE LEASH
No mess, no bother, and you never have to replace it!

**Total Cost: $49.95
(batteries not included).**

#60000000 THE MARTIN BORMANN WHITE CANE AND CATTLE PROD Originally invented during the second World War for visually handicapped Germans, this device was only available for those who could prove they saw nothing. We have adapted the original mechanism and transistorized the entire unit, so this dual purpose walking stick and cattle prod is lightweight and completely portable. Mass production allows us to offer it at this incredibly low price: only **$51.00** per unit.

Batteries available at slight additional cost. If optional adapter pack is ordered, unit recharges off car battery as well as home current.

**Total Cost: $51.00.
Batteries: $3.99 per set.
Adapter Unit: $29.95.**

**Manufactured by Cyclon B., Inc.
East and West Germany
(A Division of Kropp, Inc.)**

#89876789 **HOUSE AND GARDEN MISSILE SILO** Patriots, True-Blue Americans, help keep our country safe from International Communist Conspiracy! Install late-model missile silo in backyard (or large patio). Even if spineless government, dominated by bleeding heart liberals, abandoned these silos, our ever alert buyers snapped up every one! Complete with missile (specify: single or multiple entry), two unemployed technicians, remote control red button and advanced radar dish.

Check local zoning ordinances before installing: if they conflict, ignore them! YOU ARE THE FIRST LINE OF AMERICAN DEFENSE!

Total Cost: $755,000.00 Shipped by truck from unnamed disposal house in South Dakota. Allow six weeks for delivery.

#4681300   THE ULTIMATE JOGGER'S GIFT   Don't let the small size fool you. It's an entire gift package in lightweight nylon that attaches to the waistband, and it's all for the jogger who wishes to combine the healthy outdoor sport of running with something even more spiritually substantial. Imagine the delight as he or she unfastens this tiny packet and unfolds a waterproof, vellum map, offering directions and instructions on the ultimate running trip. By following the illuminated numbers, the jogger can actually RUN THROUGH THE STATIONS OF THE CROSS. At the completion there's also a dehydrated transubstantiation pellet included.

At this never before low price, we offer it all, a truly uplifting experience for only **$4.67.**

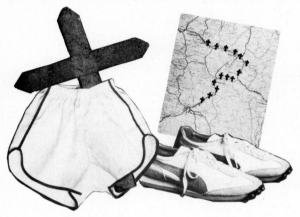

#0-12   THE HEISENBERG SPECIAL   For the amateur physicist, our exciting kit offers a range of experiments designed specifically for the 10–12 year age bracket. Included are the lesser sub-atomic particles, a small Cyclotron which has been tested and approved by our own laboratories, plus three vials of uncontaminated matter.

Watch your favorite little scientist's eyes light up as he or she manipulates the basic building blocks of our universe that change in accordance with Heisenberg's own Uncertainty Principles!

Packaged and shipped under strict supervision. We guarantee what we mail will change while you watch it.

Total Cost: $333.22 plus small handling charge. ERDA Approval Pending

#080808   GIFTS FOR LAWYERS   For those who have just passed the bar, the perfect present! Our *Judge Crater Indemnity Cloak*; fits both men and women (one size for all) and is perfect in any weather. Lightweight, waterproof, it protects the wearer in and out of court, against malfeasance, malpractice and mal de mer.
Two colors: Moot Magenta or Torte Tan, the lawyer in your life will wear it with pride and assurance.

Cloak: $19.95. Mask, extra.

F.O.B. Malibu

#10090   RUNNING/JOGGING SHOES   These sure-grip shoes were originally designed for climbing up walls, but we saw them and realized they would be perfect for anyone in a confined area, such as an apartment, sailing ship, or prison. You'll never miss a step or fall, thanks to these shoes with built-in retractable suction cups. What's more, they look EXACTLY like the high priced leather running shoes you've been paying up to $90.00 per pair to own. Ours are unbelievably reasonable at only **$5.98** a pair, and if you order two or more pairs, we throw in the laces, free, as well.

Imported from Pittsburg

#123123123 DOUBLE HELIX BELTBUCKLE NEW! Our Double Helix BeltBuckle is an exact replica of the Spiral Life Force and it quickly attaches to any size belt. Comes in simulated Gold, Bronze, Brushed Chrome, or for evening occasions: Sparkling Multi-Colored Rhinestones. **Each is only $5.95.** Interlinkage Completely Guaranteed!

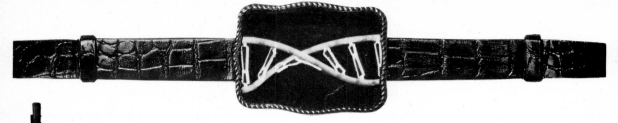

#0 POLISH GOLF CLUBS
Need we say more? Specify right or left thumb to insure perfect fit.

Price: $35.00-$40.00 each, depending on thumb.

#789011 INFLATE-A-PIMP
Give that someone who serves you something to serve him or her. As a token of your affection, what could be more thoughtful than this instantly inflatable kit which comes with foot pedal allowing it to be blown and shown in seconds!

Total Cost: In Black Vinyl $19.95

With accompanying lavender luxury convertible: $13,500.00 [accessories optional].

#96 EMPRESS DRAG QUEEN RACER The finest in custom transportation! Imagine an interior so lavish you have to see it to believe it. From the contour custom fitted denim (4-ply) and ermine seats, to the cunning dashboard in matched ultrasuede, the exquisite interior only hints at the power this beauy delivers, right under the raked hood. Five hundred magnificent brutes of horsepower, boosted into action with an amylnitrate overdrive and you're off and running. Whether it's the Greenwich 500, or just a cruise around town, this winner makes you Queen for a day. Just buckle yourself into place with your own customized rhinestone seat belts and be off!

Please specify initials when ordering. Allow 6 weeks for delivery. **Only $25,000.00 complete.**

#00890 EXPLODING WATERMELON PERFUME In its own tiny green and white striped steel vial, it's both perfume (with seeds) and an afro comb. But when you pull the pin—you do the man in! It's a gift which keeps on giving. Proved effective in South Bronx!

Total Cost: $13.66 (Please specify fragrance and mm desired).

Note: Essence of Fried Chicken is also available, with removable drumstick. Please specify regular or crispy.

#9626 PERSONALIZED CHILDREN
Lose, misplace children often? Try our system: names and license plates tattooed across forehead, buttocks for small children. Children of above-average intelligence can be taught as early as one year to emit character-istic cry.

Cry Frequencies: $99.50.
Tattooing (Crayola Type): $13.00.

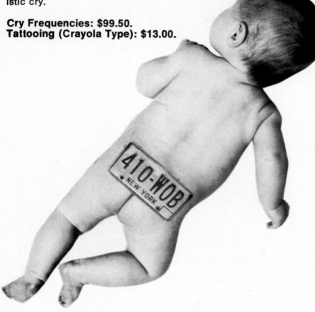

#64801 BOY SCOUT, MANUAL
Cunning life-size, highly-colored Boy Scout (key-wound) performs good deed each day, assists old ladies across streets, lights fire by rubbing sticks together (permanent sticks included), recites Boy Scout oath at time pre-selected by owner.

#64802 BOY SCOUT, AUTOMATIC
Triumph of transistorization (from our vast new electronics complex on Ob River) performs all functions of Manual Scout (above), lights fire by simply pointing at fuel with index finger, re-cites Shorter Catechism (snooze but-ton provided), plays standard bugle calls. Head tilts back to permit use as unusually striking flower vase.

#1,2,3,4,5,½ HOUSE-HOLD ELVES
Our elves eat almost nothing: large communal bowl of milk on the porch at night will do it, but each elf is trained to a special duty: vacuum-ing, dusting, washing dishes, even mending shoes. The perfect helpers for overworked parents!
   Warning: Elves work ONLY at night; attempt to make them work daytime will violate National Labor Relations Act, cause strike or curse.
   Six elves, closely matched in size and col-oration: **per week: $35.00.**

(Note: Elves NOT avail-able during Christmas Season).

#64803 BOY SCOUT, MANUEL
Same as Manual Scout (above), but recites oath in Spanish. Several interesting Spanish oaths provided.

Manual: $235.00.
Automatic: $4,400.00.
Manuel: $245.00 (includes tilda).

COURSES BY CORRESPONDENCE Anyone can become an expert. Spend just a few spare evenings each week in the privacy of your own home, actually perfecting a new line of work.

Send for our complete course instructions; choose from one of the many exciting professions which are now available! Each course comes complete with step-by-step instructions featuring color-plate illustrations and a series of taped cassettes, all developed by an expert in that particular field.

Become your own expert! Save money and costly hours! And all of it in your own home, at your own rate of speed.

BEGINNING COURSES: (Please specify one or more. Prices vary according to actual materials required. Discount for three or more courses available.)

#24	**JET PILOT TRAINING**
#74	**MICROSURGERY FOR BEGINNERS**
#75	**NEUROSURGERY AND INTESTINAL BYPASSES**
#62	**PERFECT HEART TRANSPLANTS AND HOOKUPS**

#63	**OPERATING YOUR HOME LINEAR ACCELERATOR**
#64	**NUCLEAR REACTORS AND FUSION DEVICES: A CHEAP QUICK METHOD TO HEAT YOUR HOME AND NEIGHBORHOOD**
#53	**CORPORATE LAW MADE EASY**
#69	**BECOMING A SUPREME COURT JUDGE**
#99	**RUNNING A STOCK EXCHANGE**
#91	**CITY PLANNING AND STRUCTURAL STEEL ASSEMBLAGE**
#94	**BUILDING COMMUNICATION SATELLITES**
#95	**KEEPING COMMUNICATION SATELLITES IN ORBIT**
#98	**UNDERWATER DEMOLITION AND DAM CONSTRUCTION**
#20	**SO YOU WANT TO BE AN ASTRONAUT!**
#14	**STARTING YOUR OWN COMMODITIES EXCHANGE**
#32	**SO YOU WANT TO BE A PROSTITUTE!**
#01	**GENETIC ENGINEERING AND THE HOME GARDENER**
#25	**ADAPTING THE HOME FREEZER FOR PROFIT: CRYOGENICS AND SPERM BANK FACILITIES FOR BEGINNERS**

GIFTS ON THE SLY

Purchasing power of the dollar is declining daily; for a real investment, works of art make more sense than ever. Again, we can't name these special gifts; all we can say is that millions of people have been awed by them. Truly one of a kind; your friends and neighbors will be overwhelmed!

Many countries now have stringent restrictions on exports of art treasures, religious works, national artifacts. Some of these items do, however, come on the market. We can give verbal assurance of authenticity, but nothing in writing.

#5-A From Switzerland A major alp. We can't give alp's name, but you will recognize it immediately. Perfect for the home rock-climber. **$235,000. But see below for combination bargain.**

#5-B From Scotland An important loch, with authenticated monster. Comes with one year's supply of monster food. **$750,000.**

#5-C From Norway You may have sailed up this beautiful fjord on an idyllic summer vacation. Now, have it in your own backyard. Needs backyard of approximately 1000 square miles. **$375,000.**

#5-A-B-C Or, All Three! No need to travel again; you'll have the best of both worlds, and it will be all yours. Combination alp, loch, fjord, **$999,000.90.** Shipping charges are the responsibility of purchaser. For a small additional sum, we provide insurance against international incidents. Subject to prior sale.

#5-D From Rome A very significant ceiling. We can't say more, but if you were thinking about God and Adam, you're probably right. Price negotiable, but requires vow of perpetual celibacy on part of buyer or buyer's representative. For additional fee, we supply representative.*

#5-E From India Interesting white marble temple, Persian ascendancy period. Comes complete with reflecting pool, peacocks. Purchaser must pledge substantial financial support to Indira Gandhi.*

#5-F From Mainland China After centuries of isolation, China is again an exporting nation, but no other export matches ours. Large wall, square towers at 100-yard intervals, splendid for extensive undulating terrain. "Good fences make good neighbors" said Robert Frost, and this purchase ought to make the best neighbors ever. Comes with authentic antique seal of approval from Ghengis Khan.*

#5-G From Paris Unusual open-work steel tower, platforms, elevators. Perfect as advertisement for business or for summer entertaining. Naturally, there's only one of these, but for the purchaser who looks ahead, next year we hope to offer a large seventeenth-century palace, grounds, carp pools, vicious carp. Buyer will need to install indoor plumbing, pay considerable under-cover sums to venial French government officials.*

Our third group of one of a kind On The Sly gifts, and why has nobody thought of it before: people! Our own researchers identified them, our own agents did the delicate negotiations. Nowhere but here! *

#5-H From London Well-mannered, experienced head of state. Comes with extensive wardrobe, tiaras, lovely upper-class accent. Is at home in all situations, opens bazaars beautifully. Husband can be provided if you need matched set; husband truly inexpensive.*

#5-I From Washington DC Used president, low rating in polls, perfect for family room. A fun gift to keep your guests laughing. Year's supply of tooth polish included.*

#5-J From Soviet Russia Assorted pack of twelve, includes dissenters, Jews, poets, ballet dancers (specify Bolshoi or Kirov). All come with guarantee of asylum from U.S. State Department. Translator extra, except with dancers.*

* Prices Negotiable—Subject to Prior Sale. Write For Estimate.

#50392777 PETS FOR PENNIES No home need be without a pet any longer! Thanks to this extraordinary once-in-a-lifetime offer, adorable used laboratory animals from the finest testing laboratories are now available. Enjoy having YOUR VERY OWN pet, plus OUR FULL ASSURANCE that it is one of a kind. From mutant mice to monster monkeys, just write and tell us the size area you have available and we will ship one, two or even three lovable pets right off to you.

Don't wait! We just don't know how long we'll be able to keep these in stock.

Price per pet: $.11, plus shipping and crating. (Missing parts, extra.)

GREATER LESSER AUK

#224466 LIVING GIFT Delight your favorite bird-watcher with this gift, the "Lesser Auk" for only **$25.00.** (Replaces item #224465, "Greater Auk," which has been discontinued.)

#10812 LIVING BIB Avoid embarrassment at formal dinners. Bib absorbs, lives on, spilled food, moves rapidly, is almost undetectable, can absorb even cigar ash. Easily tamed. Taupe, mauve, and flesh.

Total Cost: $75.00.

#654321 GNOME D'PLUME Ours, exclusively! French dwarf, complete with feathers (feathers in purple only).

Total Cost: $9.99.

Imported From England

#75555 PUMPKIN/MICE CONVERSION SET Beat the transportation crisis and never worry about a gas shortage again! Just place the pre-set pumpkin on your driveway, at least 20' from garage, and press the electronic hand unit. It's that easy! Pumpkin turns into full size gilded coach. Press the button again and the 6 mice (included) become full-size obedient coachmen, ready to take you wherever your heart desires.

Mice run on cheese (not included) and are fully warranteed to work during daylight and early evening hours. After midnight, entire set converts back to pumpkin/mice and should be kept in cool, dry place with adequate ventilation. If properly stored, can be reused up to lifetime of pumpkin or mice, whichever comes first.

$49.95 per set (compact models not yet available).

#594665 MATCHED RATS FOR DEDICATED YACHTSMEN Pair of brindled rats, calibrated in our laboratories to leave sinking ship one half-hour before disaster. Rats reproduce selectively: no cost beyond original investment. Female has implanted barometer; male, tiny but accurate nautical compass.

Pair: $150.00, brindling included.

Shipped from Stavanger, Norway

#000901 UGLY DUCKLINGS No need to worry that the darling Ugly Duckling you bought as a pet will predictably turn into a swan on maturity. These little creatures grow up to become SHABBY SWANS, thanks to the fact that they have been bred to molt continuously and retain that lovable fuzzy appearance.

Sold only as matched pairs (male and female), swans will breed a true strain upon reaching full adult size.

Only $300.00 per pair. Live shipment guaranteed.

#43210 DORMANT SICILIAN KILLER BEES Trouble with noisy neighbors in the summer? Warm, release our exclusive bees (average size ½ lb., queen much larger). Your troubles are at an end! Field-tested; 16 bees wiped out entire rock concert in Georgia! Sicilian phrase book with necessary commands (Fly! Dive! Return to Cryogenic Bottle!).

Basic Hive of 30 Bees: $759.00.
Extra Queen: $250.00.

#5403 CYANEA ARCTICA This remarkable jellyfish, largest known, has tentacular span up to 245', is easily domesticated, answers to name, performs simple tricks, can be persuaded to serve as tent for summer cocktail parties, weddings.

IMPORTANT: Do not order without owner's information manual that SPECIFIES THE NAME OF YOUR OWN PARTICULAR JELLYFISH! Jellyfish responds only to its own name! From waters off Bora Bora.

Basic jellyfish: $7,500.00.

#89038 HOG WASH One application makes family hog white, glistening. Spray nozzle adjusts to size of hog.

Only $4.50.

#91234 PERSONALIZED FISH Teach your child to identify with pets. Catfish or Chinook Salmon are shipped to you in leakproof containers, each monogrammed with the child's initials. Herrings and halibut also available at the same low cost of **only $9.98 per fish.**

Note: U.S. Immigration Laws specifically prohibit monogramming of Piranha in this country, so we cannot offer this variety at this time.

#213312 OPOSSUMS! WALLABIES! Sudden overstock from HELP OUR FRIENDS THE MARSUPIALS Center in Gladys, Australia. Our buyers cornered the market: 7600 furry friends that Edith Smythe-Cooke and her aborigine helpers could no longer control. No trouble to keep: Opossums feed on carrion (available in any household), Wallabies on tender Eucalyptus leaves and shoots. Watch animals hiss, spit at being observed, take babies out of pouches, nervously return babies to pouches. A laugh-treat for the whole family. And inexpensive!

Two dozen Opossums: $17.95.
One dozen Wallabies: $44.50.

Guaranteed to last 6 months even under urban stress, children.

Carriage from Australia, extra.

#0900 TOOLS FOR THE HOME INQUISITOR Relive one of history's most exciting times in the privacy of your basement or garage! We'll transform it into a compact, authentic down-to-the-last-detail DUNGEON!

Included in this Home Environment are: full-size Teflon-Coated Iron Maiden and Matching Mace (Wash and Wear guaranteed), Expando-Rack with Accompanying Tension Gauge (Luminous Digital Readout). All Arm and Leg Clamp units are completely adjustable, and each unit comes in stress-tested Blond Oak or Mahogany finish.

Early Buyer's Bonus includes Two simulated Iron Cross Bar Assemblies, One Cubic Foot of Pre-Stained Dirt, and Assorted Religious Wall Artifacts.

Total Cost: $234,220.33: plus small shipping charge beyond our 50 mile radius. SOON TO COME: Our Lazy-Duke (48″ by 96″) authentic Replica ELECTRIC GRILL UNIT. Can also double as Barbecue, for party occasions.

#0009 SWAMP Write for details.

#94219 LEDA AND THE SWAN GANG Funny home TV video-tape, shows why birds and people belong to-gether; lots of information on eggs, Greek religion.

Tape: $17.50.

LEDA AND THE SWAN GANG

#6454 HARE SHIRT Once so rare and costly that only the wealthy could afford to even dream of owning one, these Hare Shirts are now available for the first time, thanks to modern science.

We've crossed the genetically delicate New Zealand wild rabbit (not an endangered species) with its hardier cousin, the Uruguay civet, and stabilized the mutant strain to produce a lustrous fur. Hand plucked to insure color gradation and shaft tolerance, then woven on specially designed looms.

We guarantee each shirt to last an entire lifetime! Not affected by seasonal molt or weather conditions. Colors: Checker (our half-and-half), Bisque Brown (vibrant rich earth tones), Avalanche (white), and **each is available at the low price of $14.99. Two or more only $14.50 each.**

#42 ATTACK HAMSTERS A perfectly matched pair of Attack Hamsters! Bred in our German laboratories, these genetic mutations have three-inch teeth with lethal overbite. Each pair comes complete with cage, instructions for feeding and bloodmeal pellets for one month.

Attack Hamsters are perfect protectors of property and are trained to respond to attack command by silent hamster whistle (included) which also releases cage door.

Cheaper than guard dogs, these cute, furry bundles are family pets as well. Your children can cuddle them. One male and one female Hamster are shipped direct to you, and we guarantee they will breed as you watch, providing educational and preventional material, plus hours of endless delight for the entire family.

Total Cost: $445.22 per pair, plus shipping.

#43 DRAFT COCKERS These enormous red-brown Cocker Spaniels have been specifically bred for us in our Latvia headquarters to provide the perfect answer for those who feel they haven't the room for matching Clydesdale horses. Lovable cockers are well known for their extreme affection and loyalty, and with typical cocker longevity, years of guaranteed pleasure are yours with each purchase.

Total cost per Cocker: $678.00, plus crate and shipping. 500-lb. package of puppy food included. Intricate Harness, extra. Please specify color: Red-Brown or Brown-Red.

#44 THE POETS' PETS A pair of Roget's Cockatoos. From the jungles of the East Indies, a rare and almost extinct species has been discovered which we now offer in matched pairs. Birds display brilliant plumage in shades of magenta, teal green, bright orange and gray. Male cockatoo is trained to supply rhyme words in metric cadence upon command; Female, free-verse and syllabic count.

Any poet you know would more than welcome these pets; they make sonnets a snap, and free-verse an effortless delight!

**Male Cockatoo (rhyming): $44,500.90.
Female Cockatoo (free verse and syllabics): $44,500.91.**

A set of matched cockatoos: $44,500.98 plus shipping. Cage is included in this price. Please specify wicker or chrome. Binding and jesses extra.

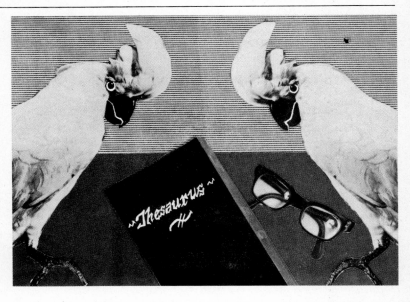

#131304 HOME FANATIC Parties not as talkworthy as you'd hoped? Fanatics, available on daily rent or long lease, can be disguised as friends, family members. Guaranteed to raise emotional temperature by minimum of 10° C. within 15 minutes; if dissatisfied, return for full refund. When not in use, fanatics must be kept on steel leash, provided.

Moderate Fanatics: $50.00 per hour.
Extreme Fanatics: $150.00.
Ultimate Fanatic model under development; available 1984.

#131311 HYBRID FARM ANIMALS Our exclusive genetic crosses. Musk-Ox-Cat (MUSKCAT) kills mice, grazes on leftover stir-fry, produces natural yogurt. Good with children. SHEEP-CARP gives good knitting wool, bones for attractive homemade combs. Other crosses in development.

    WARNING: Do not attempt natural reproduction, crosses unstable! Prices on request, shipped from our proving grounds in Utah.

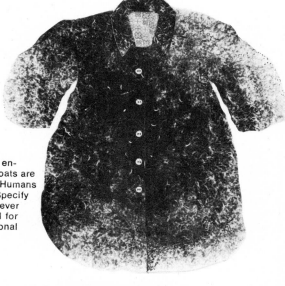

#1981 FAKE FURS No exploitation of endangered species here! Our FAKE FUR coats are made only from extremely hairy humans. Humans chosen for density and softness of hair. Specify blond, dark, redhead; we can match whatever you need. Write our consultant: Miss Seal for more information (price depends on personal choice and availability).

#84721 BICENTENNIAL TUNA Spectacular genetic manipulation produced for the bicentennial just 24 of these 200-pound tuna, each of which displays on its back, in full phosphorescent color, 13-star flag of the ORIGINAL UNITED STATES, on its belly, hand-written PREAMBLE TO THE CONSTITUTION. Most of these fish have been snapped up by the national libraries, museums; the few that remain are virtually priceless.
    Write for quotation. Not available through retail stores.

#49   THE BLACK HOLE TOUR   Nothing as common as Calcutta for you! This tour is truly a once in a lifetime, out-of-this-world adventure. Experience gravity at its finest, as you're drawn toward a selected black hole with a whole new universe on the other side. Yours, when you book early.

Tour will be scheduled to take advantage of free launch days at Vandenberg Launch site, and will be led by noted Cornell astronomer.

Total Cost: $50,000. Includes one-way ticket and all meals en route. Ticket must be paid for thirty days in advance and anti-matter waiver must be signed prior to departure.

#48   THE BRIGHAM YOUNG GROUP TOUR   Complete family entertainment package. Tour the Timpanogos Caves, Pinnacle Mountains and basin of Great Salt Lake; watch the thousands of performing sea gulls as they swoop and dive in formation. Then relax in the auditorium as the Mormon Tabernacle Choir performs selected medlies of old favorites for three hours.

Tour Cost: $555.00 plus 10% tithing. Price based on double or more occupancy; group discounts not available. No alcohol, caffeine or other stimulants will be permitted ERA advocates excluded.

#77   OUR ST. ANTHONY DELUXE 'GET STONED IN PUBLIC PLACES' TOUR   For the novice martyr or the genuinely dissatisfied, this tour is once again available. It includes your choice of 14 public marketplaces, an aroused citizenry (complete with stones) and the once-in-a-lifetime opportunity to partake in an ancient ritual. This tour replaces one previously offered, titled "Lottery Tour."

Tour Package, including one-way ticket: $3,221.00. Includes visas and togas, which we furnish, at no additional cost.

#49   MAKE YOUR MARK IN MOVIES   Fly to glamorous Hollywood where three movie sets are waiting for your firsthand introduction into the art of filmmaking. Tour commences with work on the epic remake of classic *Pele, Queen of the Volcanoes* with actual human sacrifices by starlets.

Next, on location in San Diego, you'll work and mingle with the cast and crew of *I Was A Teenage Komodo Dragon* as they recreate Java, down to the last sultry detail using authentic straw mini-skirts and actual venom. You'll learn how Komodo dragons are trained to simulate devouring teenagers and which

camera angles are used in close-up drowning shots.

Before the tour ends, you will have an additional chance to put all this new knowledge into working practice, on location at sea for the filming of *Goodbye, Dr. Flips.* Enjoy lunch with the young starlet who falls in love with the aging dolphin, and over tuna salad, she'll explain to you how she has been taught to interpret the dolphin's desires. Optional tour (with lunch) available to visit dolphin.

Total Cost: $6,000.00. This includes all meals, except optional fish lunch with dolphin.

#0000 OUR REJECTING TYPEWRITER, The "Univerb Self-Correcting IV" Been party to an indiscretion, written something you wish you hadn't? Never again, as our "Univerb Self-Correcting IV" is programmed to take the worry out of being prose. A technological miracle from one of America's finest monopolies, the tiny computer, heart of the machine, assumes full and total responsibility for everything you write. Phrase after phrase of utmost, inoffensive and forgettable language means you never regret what you shouldn't have written. The Univerb IV won't permit you to write it!

The total cost of this tested and approved typewriter is $38,000.00 plus local tax. Includes carbon ribbons, and full one year warranty on all unmoving parts. Software extra.

#78432 IDI AMIN SOLAR HOT TUB Uninvited guests, colleagues, family members are NO TROUBLE TO ENTERTAIN when you introduce them to THE ULTIMATE HOT TUB! No wiring, no insulation. Powerful solar generators raise water temperature to 178° C in minutes. Troubles evaporate!

Two models: Temperate Zone, from Trondheim, **$7,200.00** uses fresh Norwegian spring water.

Equatorial, from Entebbe, more durable, uses glycerin; in emergency can run on melted animal fat. **$12,750.00.**

(Ayatollah Khomeini Model will be available later in the year, when and if shipments resume.)

#8700 THE MARIE CELESTE II TOUR Feel the need to escape winter weather? This tour is designed with you in mind as it allows you the chance to relax on board our special sailing vessel, the *Marie Celeste II*. With your carefully chosen shipmates, you'll spend your days enjoying the bright sun as you sail away toward Bermuda, and by mid-ocean you'll feel your cares slipping away in the congenial atmosphere. This tour includes everything from souvenir triangle, suitably inscribed with your name, to your very own life-preserver, monogrammed with your initials.

Tour cost: $1,467.99. Payable in advance. Not refundable.

#990 OUR TWO-DAY, SEVENTEEN-NIGHT TOUR OF BUFFALO AND ERIE Starting in January, we're delighted to be able to offer this old favorite again. For all of our surviving customers who requested it and whom we had to disappoint when the airport and surrounding facilities were closed due to blizzards, this sought after trip is now available.

We begin (as in previous years) with a special dinner at the Buffalo airport. After this unforgettable experience, places have been reserved in the waiting and lounge areas where we'll gather to be whisked off to Erie. There, the group will tour the wine vats just under the canal. This exciting once-a-year tour always fills early, so be sure to mail your deposit right off to "Shuttle-Off-To-Buffalo."

Price of Tour: $672.44. This includes tax, tip, and decompression.

#52 A GOURMET TOUR OF PHILADELPHIA For you, your chosen companion and personal physician, we offer once again the Gourmet Tour of Philadelphia, which features the City of Brotherly Love at its finest. Restaurant selection is only made public an hour before departure, so a genuine surprise is in store for the three of you!

Price of Tour: $3.98 (Minus tax and gratuities. Totally deductible. Monogrammed stomach pump available at slight extra cost.)

#609468 THE NEW JERSEY SPE-CIAL or BLACK HAND TOUR Thanks to the magic of Mafia, we're able to offer this tour that begins in the casinos at Atlantic City where a gift coupon entitles you to 14 nickels for $10.00 and a chance to play the slot machines. Following your gala evening, you'll leave the next morning for scenic Newark, where a complete refinery tour has been arranged with lunch al fresco on the sidewalk.

Our tour continues to nearby Secaucus and then on to Camden, Haddonfield and selected spots on the New Jersey Turnpike. During the course of the tour, fine Italian meals will be provided and eaten. Cement shoes optional.

Price of Tour: $17.92. This includes kick-backs, bribes, and all payoffs. Transportation, lodging, and meals extra.

#44 OUR "YOU LEFT YOUR HEART IN CHICHEN-ITZA" TOUR This repeat of our ever popular tour is yours, when you send your volunteer contribution, in our name, to your local Public Broadcasting Station. Thanks to another government grant with matching funds, this low price includes everything!

Tour Cost: $31.00. This includes one-way ticket and sacrificial robe.

#45 SUMMER SOLSTICE AT STONEHENGE TOUR For a select group of thirteen, we once again make available this fantastic tour. Set your watch as the sun makes its annual angular approach at Stonehenge and then draw straws as the lucky volunteer is selected to participate in the ancient Druid rites, which guarantee fertility, annual rainfall and a good crop of sports cars.

Total Cost: $1,354.00 plus tax. Waiver must be signed prior to departure for you to receive your authorized one-way ticket.

#67495867 MACOMBER TOUR Hunters, natural killers—hard to find a new thrill these days? Our 24-day full guided tour allows you to endanger as many as six species (pygmy rhinoceros extra). Guns provided, but you pay for expanding bullets.

Macomber tour, travel, hotels, meals, starts $25,000, double occupancy. Refund if mate lost.

#901 TOUR DE FORCE Excitement in a semi-tropical or tropical climate! You'll be where the action is, right on the front lines as the soccer game erupts into a revolution, or on the oil fields as the production slows down and the troops leave to quell the newest insurrection. This tour has been arranged especially for those retired Army, Navy, Marine Corps or officers from foreign countries whose leisure time seemed endless, until now. Relive the actual moments of hand-to-hand combat with your foreign counterparts! Advise the junta on new plans of attack!

Interpreters will be on hand to translate subtleties and explain changes in command as they happen.

Total Tour: $6,000. Disclaimer waiver must be signed and own armament must be furnished.

#7777 FOR THE SOPHISTICATE Done everything? Seen all there is to see? For the sophisticate who has reached the point of no return, we can offer the ultimate trip: *An Alternative Universe!*

It's more than something a bit out of the way, it's completely out of this world! You may find the rules of gravity don't apply, and cause and effect have been nullified in one of the Alternative Universes. In another, you'll find anti-matter provides you with a backward look at your life, as you grow younger each year you stay. And stay you will!

It's not a trip for the timid, but it is THE trip for the person who has tried everything and wants even more.

Write for complete details, bus schedules and probable dates of departure. Sorry, no family rates apply on this one. All you've never expected and more!

#009 OUR AGNOSTIC SPECIAL TOUR For those who bring to every occasion their own sense of despair, what better place to get away from it all than on a tour designed especially for you? We take you to Tierra Del Fuego, on the ultimate survival cruise, and for an entire week, you are cast onto the shores to survive, naked, with the elements against you. Test your lack of faith in the terrible volcanic regions. Climb the glacial outcroppings and be battered by torrential storms! (Included at no extra cost.) And if you survive, come back and tell us all about it; we'll book you on a money-making tour of the continent. So either way, you can't lose more than your lack of faith!

Total Cost: $400.87, plus any and all credit cards, signed to our Captain.

#60006　THE ELGIN MARBLES　As is.

F.O.B. Greece. Transhipped via London.

Price Seasonal
Sealed Bids Only, Please.

#080706　HALF TRACK WHEELCHAIR　Go anywhere, in any season, as wilderness and rugged mountain terrain are no match for this totally self-contained baby! Front wheel drive puts positive action into the two oversize wheels, mounted in WW II surplus tank tread.

Revolving turret swivels a full 360 degrees for big game hunting and the E-Z reach gun rack allows instant access for all equipment, from rifles, bazookas, to fishing har-poons. Brushed chrome or plain armor plate; tested in actual combat situations; all moving parts guaranteed. Tread, motor components and detachable lasers fully warranted for one year. Veteran loans arranged with financing approved by all government agencies.

Total Cost: $5,999.00 plus small shipping surcharge.
F.O.B. Tehran

#131307 SPACE-A-FAMILY Somebody on your block need a real rest, and you too? Our skilled technicians will stun, wrap and anesthetize, and then it's into orbit in a carefully designed polystyrene capsule. Order two adults, and children under twelve fly free. Vicious pets extra. Available only on special order: specify family name, number of occupants, Social Security number.

#30988 REVERSIBLE LEI From Vanda to Venus with just a quick flick of the wrist! What a way to greet returning travelers or as a perfect send-off for those going to exotic places! Vanda orchids on one side, Venus fly traps on the other of this exquisitely hand-strung floral garland.

Live shipment guaranteed and gift boxed, of course.

Total Cost: $9.98 plus shipping. Flies not included.

#290 PHRASEBOOK OF   INSULTS
For those moments which should   be matched insult for insult, this complete phrasebook is essential for the traveler. Translated from standard Polish, includes wide range of ethnic insults, from beginning slurs on family origin to complex curses for entire households, pets and children.

Seventy-five basic insults are provided; cover a complete range of domestic and governmental situations.

Total Cost: $9.95. (Supplement for transportation situations such as streetcars, subways or Central Park, $1.00 additional).

#46232 THE HADDON-HESSMAN LIP Molded in high-Impact phlegm, upper lip is perfect *bon voyage* gift for friends traveling to England. Three degrees of stiffness: Country Gentry, Regimental, House of Lords. Miniaturized acoustic tubes transform even the *patois* of the South Bronx into cultivated Oxbridge accent. AA Battery, not included. Stiffness determines price.

CG Model: $150.00.
R. Model: $185.00.
HL Model: $495.00 (Includes mock robes)

BONUS OFFER! With purchase of three or more Haddon-Hessman Lips, free paperback copy of current English bestseller, *How To Make Your Chin Recede.*

Country Gentry   Regimental   House of Lords

#131302 TRAVEL WITH ASSURANCE Special helps to make your trip a success wherever you go. Italy: Artificial Kneecaps, $29.95. Iran: Koran Computer, Prayer Rug, $295.00. Northern Ireland: Ideologic Defuser, $77.90. France: Insolence Gauge, $375.00. Special Deluxe Hotel Model, $779.00.

We're constantly extending this line: ask about any country and let us give you a quotation.

SUMMER SPECIAL: Boredom Kit for the Andaman Islands, only $18.90.

#289 STEREO SOUNDSPELLER Arrive at any destination with a true sense of fluency! Our handy set of six tapes teaches anyone the correct spelling of 5000 commonly misspelled words and phrases. Each word is spelled out slowly and distinctly in stereo, with pauses to allow you to repeat, letter by letter, the approved and correct spelling for the region in which you happen to be traveling.

These tapes are available in French, English, Serbo-Croatian, High Church Slavonic and Anglican, plus Russian dialects.

Complete set of six tapes only $29.95.
Fits any 8-track or stereo cassette player.
Please specify which.

Approved by AA

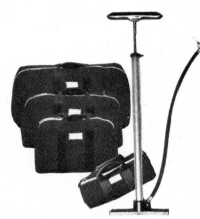

#4500 INFLATABLE LUGGAGE A size for every vacation, from the smallest 12" inflatable cosmetic case to the largest 52" carryall family luggage. You just unsnap, unroll and inflate, and pump with any bicycle pump to desired size. One size expands to fit all needs and comes in choice of finishes: clear vinyl for the neat packer, nonglare simulated black patent leather for those carrying "delicate" items. We've road-tested this baby and not one puncture in 18,000 miles. **$55.67 per unit. Not guaranteed at altitudes over 42,000 feet**

#33099 FROM FLO AND ERNIE'S LIZARD RANCH Our elegant touch-tone lizard. A Matching Set of Simulated Lizard Briefcase, Overnight Case and 48" Pullman. Goes anywhere with you, and Pullman comes complete with claw wheels and tug-along strap.

A wonderful travel idea for people on the go! All yours for only $69.95 in a choice of colors: Iguana Green, Komodo Brown, or Salamander Silver.

Monogrammed at slight additional cost. Please allow three weeks for monogramming.

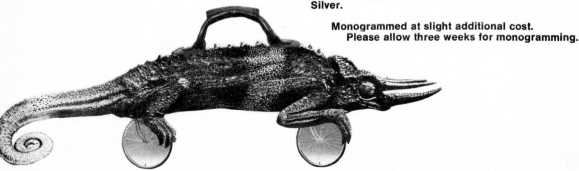

#978 OUR MOSLEM SPECIAL This "Live Prayer Rug" will follow your Moslem friends anywhere in the world. Genuine live green algae have been mutated (successfully) in our own laboratories on the Orkney Islands to completely resemble the finest Persian weavings, even while in motion. So there is no need for your Moslem friends to pack their own prayer rugs; our number follows right along, anywhere; attacks infidels.

Total Cost: $32.76 (At slight extra cost, a self-timing prayer call and compass, guaranteed to point to correct direction of Mecca, can be installed, Minarets not included.)

#8421 FOR YOUR EQUESTRIAN FANCIER Make the next hunt something memorable! Just let us know at least three weeks ahead of time and we'll ship to you THE FOUR HORSEMEN. We guarantee you've never seen riding like this!

Total Price (includes costumes and appropriate regalia): $6,789.01 for all four. Sorry, this comes as a complete package; all or nothing.

#45 PIGSKIN MEZUZAH The perfect gift for your Jewish friends who are torn between assimilation and Gommorrah. Mezuzah contains entire Talmud, printed on thinnest pigskin, to nail on the doorposts of their house, gate. It will delight any family you know who is trying to enter the right country club or acceptable neighborhood.

Total Cost: $15.77. Includes gift card and mailing.

#8469 FULL MOON SPECIAL Your very own werewolf hunt. Please specify when full moon is to occur in your area and we'll ship you via railway express all the essentials for your gala moonlight hunt. Wolfbane, silver bullet, and Field Guide for North American Lycanthropes are included, plus one genuine werewolf. If package arrives early, werewolf has been trained to simulate English peerage and can be utilized at pre-hunt party to entertain guests.

Total Price: 750 guineas per kill.

#3309   VAT-A-TROMP   Our best selling kit available once more for wine buffs who wish to explore fine art of making wine. Included are genuine Barolo grapes, one native Italian (Piemontese: not over 4'7") with own year supply of garlic (crushed cloves) and a genuine wooden vat. In addition, we supply personalized labels ("Another Vintage Year Pressing From The _____ Vintners").

Total Cost: $5,689.00. This includes tax and one-way transportation from Bergamo, Italy. Please specify correct spelling for labels.

Caution: Green work card not provided for native Italian. Check local immigration laws in your area.

#3333   CONVERTA GRILL-'N-BUMPER   Anyone can have personalized license plates, only you have the satisfaction of owning custom GRILL-'N-BUMPER molded to your exact specifications. Send automobile parts, photo of loved one, pet. We create complete likeness from photo, and living sculpture is returned to you, ready to install on front of car.

Drive in gleaming chrome splendor, loved one or pet leading way, testimony to your taste.

Total Cost: $5,222.00 including tax, plain brown wrapper, rust-proofing and shipping. Impact-resistant rubber absorbers, extra.

HAVE WE GOT A PARTY FOR YOU!!

Tired of the same old parties with the same old boring themes? With the help of our party crew and catering service, we can make your next party one they'll all remember for a lifetime or three weeks, whichever comes first.

Here's just a partial sample of what we can do for you. **Write for prices.**

#43201   THE DONNER PARTY   This genuine historical theme demands no special dress; just have your guests come as they are. We'll whisk them away via helicopters to a pre-selected mountain site where the party commences. They won't even have to bring their favorite pets, as we include a random sampling of burros, oxen, and dogs at no extra cost. It's the ultimate in wilderness parties and one we're sure they'll talk about for as long as they live. For reasons of authenticity, this party is only offered after first snowfall.

#43202   THE CONSERVATIVE PARTY   Mopeds are included in this one, and your guests will adore tooling around in their furnished robes and wigs along with you. A plastic gavel for each party-goer is included; it's just the thing for the next bar convention to wow them!

#43203   A NECKTIE PARTY   If your neighborhood's undergoing integration, we suggest this party will get things off to a flying start.

#43204   PARTY OF THE FIRST PART   This narcissistic adventure is just for one person; we include large lake for looking into, tape recorder for listening to oneself, and admiring glances.

#43205   PARTY OF THE THIRD PART   This party is one you'll go to any distance not to attend.

#43206   OFFENDED AND/ OR INJURED PARTY   Don't sulk because you weren't invited. Get even. Let us help you do it. This party is always custom-made with appropriate theme to the occasion.

#43207   PRESIDENTIAL PARTY   Includes alcoholic relative, nearsighted child and empty, flagrant promises. Guaranteed to lull even the heartiest insomniac to a state of nirvana or sleep.

#554433 KNOW AND IDENTIFY YOUR FOLLICLES Tiny micro-knife, map, plastic collecting bottles let you know and display individual follicles from your own scalp, other epidermal, pubic areas. Place follicle on sterile slide, identify and label, make lovely groupings of slides in china-cabinet or on plate-rack. Slides can be enlarged, framed for presentation to loved ones, used for unique Christmas cards.

**Follicle Identification Book: $27.50.
Scalp Map, Pubic Map: Each $4.00.
Slides: $17.50 Per Dozen.
Christmas Kit: $783.00 (includes
enlarger, gilt ink, poinsettia stickers).**

#978653 PAINT BY NUMBERS, FIRST TIME IN BRAILLE! What makes this kit UNIQUE is our Patented Color Sensor. Slip electronic gloves (nonallergenic) over your hands, activate Big Boy Color Computer. Picture is flashed instantly to brain cells, but your fingers do the work, without THOUGHT, without PREVIOUS TALENT! Just sit back and LET THEM GO! Completed oil picture emerges in micro-seconds.

Four programs now available: Winston Churchill, Grandma Moses (perennial favorite), Van Gogh Sunflowers, Currier and Ives Household Pets. In preparation: El Greco, Selected Spanish Crucifixions.

**Complete system with any one program: $11,750.00.
Additional programs: $350.00.**

#7997 THE CARGO CULT KIT Comes complete with one knocked-down, ready to assemble, plywood DC-3, and a PVC mock-up structure resembling a native hut. The full life-size dayglo God (who appears as a World War II Aviator) comes fully assembled In the box, as does a giant clam, guaranteed 4' in diameter across upper shell. A barrel of mixed barracuda and two killer sharks are also included.

Total Kit Cost: $77,087.00.

For those who wish an extra touch of realism, we can provide at a small additional cost, 6 assorted, small, yellow male models, pre-programmed to speak only Japanese. Write for price list.

**Made in Hong Kong
Assembled in Taiwan**

#34567 THE PROMETHEUS GAME For the solitary gambler, this new game includes rock, simulated liver, and gold-plated chains. A self-timer and delayed-action dedication plaque are also included. Victim and vulture must be supplied by owner.

Total Cost: $556.91 plus local tax. Please specify choice of basalt, granite, or alluvial rock.

Shipping of rock, F.O.B., Athens.

#09 DO-IT-YOURSELF TAXIDERMY KIT

Got a favorite pet or nephew you'd like to keep just that way? Our Do-It-Yourself Taxidermy Kit, "The A-To-Z, Ins-And-Outs of Taxidermy" booklet, provides easy step-by-step instructions and illustrations. Actual photos are included, showing life-like poses.

From lampshades to lampreys, everything that can be stuffed or mounted is depicted here, just as it is actually done in the finest Tijuana Tuck and Roll studios.

Tools, wooden stands, and brass plaques, suitable for engraving, are all included. Glass covers extra.

Cost of Kit: 5,000,000 pesos. This includes all taxes, border clearances, and officials' fees.

#6981209 B. FRANKLIN ELECTRICAL KITE

Teaches children of all ages principles of electricity. Requires thunderstorm (not included). Not recommended for children under 6 unless equipped with three-prong cord or adapter. SAFETY FIRST: ALWAYS GROUND CHILDREN!

$17.50, from Philadelphia.

#6981210 B. FRANKLIN SEXUAL KITE

Teaches children or maladjusted adults principles of sexuality. From Paris. Price on request; please specify age, degree and kind of maladjustment.

★ ★ ★ ★ ★ ★ ★ ★ ★ ★ ★ ★

#131313 SCARS AND STRIPES FOREVER

For the patriotic all-American masochist. Complete set features lacerating bugle, wrap-around flag impregnated with irritant compounds, reversible saluting cannon. Shipped only under-cover of night from Fort McHenry, Georgia; opens with simple Key.

$150 U.S. currency.
Ask for special rates on blood money.

★ ★ ★ ★ ★ ★ ★ ★ ★ ★ ★ ★

#50987 TAROT CARDS

Tired of telling fortunes with the same old TAROT CARDS? Ours come with TV personalities: Walter Cronkite as Emperor, Barbara Walters as Queen of Swords, Jimmy Carter as Tower Rising and Falling. Our own maintenance contract; if figure disappears from TV for 6 months, new card mailed to you absolutely free. Cards have slick, easy-to-shuffle surface.

Full Deck: $17.99.

#551 **A SOLAR ECLIPSE** Please specify
duration and type (full or partial) of
eclipse desired. Prices vary according to
season and latitude.
   Write for details.

Approved by N A S A

65768 OUR EGYPTIAN MEASURING KIT: LITER AND ASWAN Originally developed to convert the base dimensions of pyramids to rectilinear architectural proportions for tract homes, this item can also be used in the kitchen to measure flour, butter and silo grainage.

Total Cost: $567.99. F.O.B., Alexandria.

#333333 AUGURY KIT Predict tomorrow, next month, even NEXT YEAR with our exclusive AUGURY KIT. No need to disembowel loved animals or birds; we sell sterilized, reusable entrails which keep in the freezer for months. Startle friends with accuracy of your predictions!

All entrails scrupulously tested for predictive quality.

From Rome: Kit $85.00, disassembled.

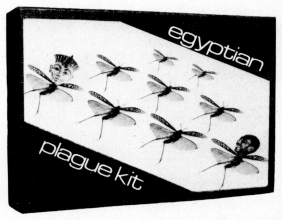

#55334 THE EGYPTIAN PLAGUE KIT Ten assorted plagues! This genuine replica includes: death of firstborn, locusts, and small rain of blood, among its many items.

Total Cost: $56.73, plus shipping and instructions on easy to assemble plague directions.

Available at slight additional cost is an accompanying kit with instructions for parting of Red Sea, for those who desire it. Please write for details.

#2222 THE CLEOPATRA SPECIAL Robe, Crown, and assorted Immortal Yearnings are included in this kit. Robe is of 100% pure Egyptian cotton, inlaid with semi-precious stones. Crown has matching motif with adjustable head band. Assorted Immortal Yearnings are packaged 12 per bottle; refills available upon request.

Total Cost: $5,000 (Asp not included due to recent FDA ruling).

#2104 OUR DOLL HOUSE Designed by Ibsen, this house comes complete with all furnishings in cluding tiny pistol and holster.
Please specify color choice: Suburban White, Urban Brown, or Rural Green.

Total Cost: $125.00, plus shipping charges from Scandinavia.

#131309 HIDING: LEARNING GAME FOR ALL AGES
Learn schizophrenia, advanced paranoia, autistic behavior, creative lying. Winner achieves complete psychosomatic withdrawal. Clever pieces to move: Foetal Curl, Hysterical Syndrome, etc. Don't go to jail, go to womb. Lead board; playing pieces degrade easily.

From our exclusive factory at Gouffe Martel: $27.50.
Contribution to International Psychoanalytic Society optional.

#000-3 THE ARMY CORPS OF ENGINEERS EASY TRAINING GAME Angered by sickly Commie ecologists? Sick of seeing innocent fish-laden streams? With our game, you turn small creeks to raging cement troughs, disrupt spawning grounds, dredge harbors and rivers to provide torrential run-offs. Heavy machinery can inundate swamps, destroy breeding grounds, bird sanctuaries. Be responsible to no one: corrupt environment at your own leisure. All benefits of modern technology in one easy training.

Total Cost: $2.49, includes tax and appropriate insignia. This game is not guaranteed for Mississippi and Athabasa Rivers. Bulldozers and heavy equipment extra.

#424334 OUR OWN SAWTOOTH FRISBEE Steel frisbee, edges honed and tempered. Teaches children caution, use of hands. Comes with or without set of hockey-type gloves.

Without Gloves: $7.50.   **With Gloves: $27.50.**

See accompanying warranty for information about prostheses.

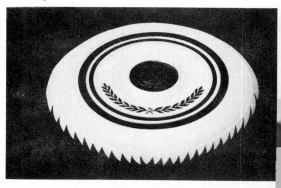

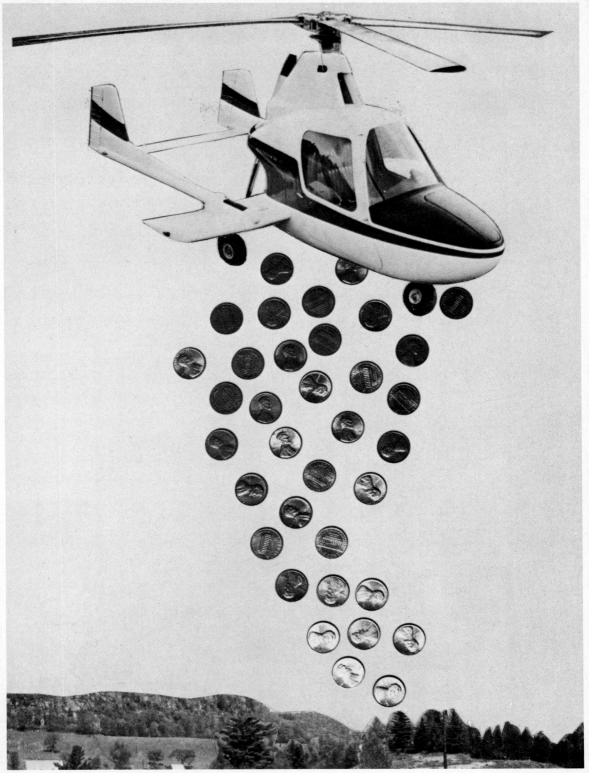

#01 PENNIES FROM HEAVEN For that special birthday, anniversary, gaily colored helicopter will hover over your lawn, shower pennies on festive guests. Amusing construction workers' hard hats provided, adhesive letters to identify occasion, can be re-used. FOR THE ULTIMATE CELEBRATION, shower guests with Susan B. Anthony dollars. Helicopter and crew, **$200.00** per hour; 5,000 pennies, **$250.00;** or: 5,000 dollars, only **$7,500.00.** Upon approved credit (bank references required) guests can be showered with Swiss Francs.

SMALL DELICACIES FROM OUR GOURMET CORNER

#1534 MOOSE HOOVES in Aspic For the True Gourmet.
#198234 DRIED YETI Called by some, "The Ultimate Aphrodisiac."
#5512 ESSENCE OF SASQUATCH Our Japanese import, reputed to be as heady as Yeti.
#12 MARSUPIAL POUCHES Stuffed with figs, or dried Australian apricots. The perfect pick-me-up.
#24 SATIVA An exotic Garlic liqueur, we capture the milky taste of each clove, then steep it for months on the high slopes of Mt. Abora in bee-skeps dating from the time of Alexander the Great.
#4 HYBRIS A delightful, heady Greek wine vinegar, made by the monks from the juices of the Nemesis Berries, according to a secret recipe handed down from the Original House of Agamemnon.
#5541 BEAR MEAT JERKY Our own smokehouse recipe.
#1234 ASSORTMENT OF EXOTIC SPICES A complete selection, including our own "Mercuree" which adds zing to the fish dish of your choice. Also included in this assortment are two jars of powdered Amanita mushrooms: an angelic touch for any dish.
#7654 USED SASHIMI
#3411 MERMAID ROE Ours exclusively.
#66 COUNTESS BORGIA'S CANNED COCKTAILS A complete assortment.
#47K KRAKATOA CHILE Hot enough to take the roof off. A *must* for the Chili aficionado.
#00 SATORI BREAD Expands your consciousness, not your waist. One slice gives you your bread. Wheat,

#1534

#24

#12

#7654

#47K

e, oleander flour, combine with alfalfa juice for all
utritional requirements. This bread had to be seen to be
chieved. Wrapped in its own mantra, imported from
epal.

901 **NOSE SCONES** An ethnic treat.

903 **LADYFINGERS** (Real).

902 **SARCOPHAGUS CAKE** To sweeten those sad
ccasions. A delicate Gateau, this cake comes completely
ecorated with all the necessary information. When
rdering, please include date of birth, demise, complete
ame of departed.

OR THE DIETER, WE INCLUDE THESE DELICACIES

22282 **PUPPY FAT** The perfect way to shed unwanted
alories. 8-ounce jar should be kept under refrigeration

when not in use. Container is reusable and decorative.

#01 MONGOLIAN CHICKEN NAVELS The quickest
and safest way to permanent weight loss. Completely safe.
Easy. Tasteless.

#02 BREASTS OF CAMEMBERT Literally, the heart of
our own process cheese. Finest ingredients blended. No
cholesterol, low in polyunsaturate cellulose.

#03 IMITATION SOY LOLLIPOPS For those who crave
a bit of sweetness, our no-cal soy suckers are superb.
Choice flavors: Sweet, Bittersweet, or Unsweetened.

#04 IMPALA ROE Our fastest moving spread; it tastes
exactly like the real thing, but without the fattening additives. Superb on Granola.

#05 SALAMANDER SAUCE Gives that needed lift to the
dieter who desires a hot, spicy sauce for fish dishes and
salads.

#903

#04

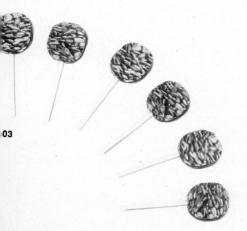

03

#090708 MCMURDO MINTINGS From our McMurdo Mint, profile faces of ALL great Antarctic explorers coined in stabilized elephant seal blubber; obverse of coin shows detailed map of tourist attractions, Mount Erebus, etc. near South Pole.

First coin shipped with intricate whalebone display rack; additional coins come once a month until all Antarctic explorers have been exhausted. Not shipped in certain months above certain latitudes: Inquire. **Price per coin: $83.50.** (Note: Coins cannot be returned if melted).

#121212 THE LUIGI J. TAMBOURINI PASTA MAKER
Executive V.P. suggested this pasta maker to our Italian chemists and Danish engineers. We offer their combined results in this stainless steel and paper alloy machine. Makes homemade pasta in just minutes out of kitchen leftovers; converts stews, soups, old salads, pies and cakes into delicate, super fine pasta. Two interchangeable blades to create ravioli, linguini, fettucini or Antonioni.

Total Cost: $5,901.23, plus tax and small shipping surcharge. F.O.B. Milan

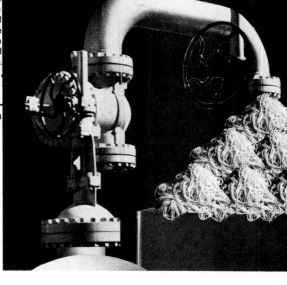

#1980 COINS FOR INVESTORS Invest in most durable currency in the world! STONE COINS FROM YAP! All hand chipped, perforated for carrying pole (not included). Easily transported by four bearers, coins cost $7.50 per Troy Ounce (average weight 850 lbs.). Shipped via Copra Schooners; please allow 18 months for delivery. AND REMEMBER: YAP HAS NOT DEPRECIATED ITS CURRENCY FOR OVER 1700 YEARS!

#1980½ NEW ACCESSORY! Four matched bearers, male, each 5'10" to 5'11", 325 to 350 lbs. Easy to domesticate, eat fish, preserved copra (see below). **Set: $130,000.00 includes all necessary papers.**

#1980-(a) PRESERVED COPRA. Exotic outer husk of coconuts steeped in lye, pummeled to rich velvety texture. A low-calorie delight with cocktails. **20-pound tin, $399.95.**

All items on this page shipped F.O.B. our warehouse in Bora Bora.

#4892038 SWAMP GUMBO Our own mixture of Okra, Mangrove Root, Blind Shrimp from deep limestone caves, Filets of Bat. Serve with Evangeline Sauce (below). 6 eight-ounce cans, $17.50. GUMBO HAS BEEN TESTED BY LOUISIANA DEPARTMENT OF AGRICULTURE AND IS GUARANTEED NOT RABID.

#1268745 MOTHER'S MUSH Trouble getting your pre-school child to eat? Our Mush is pre-chewed and partially digested in Alaska, regurgitated into sterile containers, flash-frozen, shipped directly to you in dry ice. Flavors: Whale, Seal, Caribou. DO NOT ACCEPT COMPETITORS' POLAR BEAR FLAVOR: VITAMIN A TOXIC. Dozen nipple-topped bottles: **$65.00. Shipped direct from Nome.**

#677667 CLABBER Dull, understated gift pots of CLABBER, our newest Gourmet discovery! Clabber comes from cows positively tested for Bang's disease (Bovine Tuberculosis); pots made unintentionally by welfare recipients. It's one of those happy accidents, and we have the whole supply! **Pint pot of Clabber, $7.50; quart pot, $11.00.** For someone you really want to please, CLABBER OF THE YEAR CLUB; write for specifications. All Clabber from Philadelphia and environs.

#3998 SAVORY WOOD CHIPS Why eat cholesterol-loaded potato chips when wood is slimming? Wafer-thin slices of pine, Douglas fir, cottonwood, all deep-fried and packaged in wood-finished containers. And more! 10% of profits go to the National Forest Service for its fund on re-seeding.

Fifteen ounce container: $12.75. Shipped from Yosemite, Yellowstone, Black Hills: whichever is nearest.

#3234 DOG JELLY Famous French chefs cook down a whole carcass of beef to arrive at a tiny pot of *viande*. Now try our delicious viande, concentrated through *seven days continuous reduction* in our patented stills, for those cuisines (Chinese, Mexican) which customarily eat dogs. Cover your smallest fingernail with a thin film of Dog Jelly: smell, taste! If you can't INSTANTLY identify the brand of dog involved, your money back and no questions. Currently available: Samoyed, Chihuahua, Lhasa Apsos, Keeshond (spicy flavor, best used with stews, ragouts). All dogs from AKC strains. If you have a dog you are fond of, write; he may be in our laboratories now. **One gram: $100.**

#55255 BELUGA CAVIAR FROM YOUR OWN SWIMMING POOL! Troubled by high cost of this rarest of gourmet pleasures? Our own domesticated sturgeons, bred from purest Caspian Sea Stock, are trained to produce continuous supply of roe, package it in decorative North Iranian pottery jars. YOUR OWN NAME ON LABEL: Sturgeons write name with mouth-held pens; not more than 24 characters per line, three lines. **$2750** per running foot of sturgeon: sizes 8 to 18 feet available. Fish trained to resist chlorine, guaranteed affectionate with children.

#4892039 EVANGELINE SAUCE Smooth, unctuous, a religious experience in itself. Official blessings from 17 parishes. Ingredients secret, but uses all resources of hidden bayous. **1.75 liter container: $25.00** Alcoholic content approximately 125 proof.

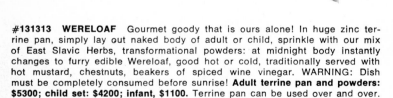

#131313 WERELOAF Gourmet goody that is ours alone! In huge zinc terrine pan, simply lay out naked body of adult or child, sprinkle with our mix of East Slavic Herbs, transformational powders: at midnight body instantly changes to furry edible Wereloaf, good hot or cold, traditionally served with hot mustard, chestnuts, beakers of spiced wine vinegar. WARNING: Dish must be completely consumed before sunrise! **Adult terrine pan and powders: $5300; child set: $4200; infant, $1100.** Terrine pan can be used over and over.

#48481 BABAS-AU-RHUM, THE LAST WORD IN DESSERTS If you *really* want to eat, why play around with kiddy recipes? Our original *babas*, made for us on an unnamed island in the Lesser Antilles, are 97% pure 165 proof Caribbean rum, and only three percent dough: just barely enough to hold the flamboyant dessert together. Packaged in heavy stoneware crocks; tap lightly with a hammer, watch the container split in half and the *baba* burst into flame WITHOUT EVEN A MATCH. One dozen *babas*, $245. (Please order early: due to international shipping regulations, these delicate confections cannot be sent through the Panama Canal.)

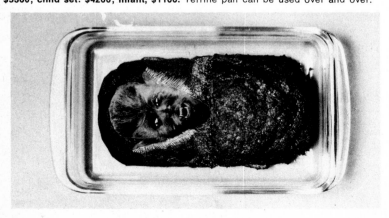

MARY BAKER EDDY YEAST

#4010000 MARY BAKER EDDY SELF-GENERATING YEAST Perfect buns each and every time with our packets of self-generating yeast. Just mix and add water, then watch as it rises! Yeast never grows old!

Price per box (each box contains four packets) $1.21.

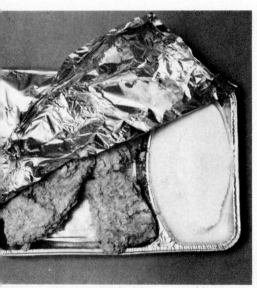

#00981 AIRLINE MEALS Why pay exorbitant costs to fly and eat? Pre-packed trays offer the convenience of meals you'd receive on transatlantic or intercontinental flight. Strip away the aluminum foil cover to reveal the steaming contents.

Selection includes main courses: reshaped meat *du jour,* boiled Erie carp over assorted vegetables, steamed fowl (this item varies according to migratory season, but is always prepared in our own turbo jet ovens for authenticity). Exciting side dishes: crumbly potatoes, parsley salad with beans. Puddings: blood, tapioca, or instant.

For bigger eaters, our *Concorde Special,* a revolutionary concept: complete meal, heated and eaten in 10 seconds. Fast-moving tray includes giant portions of escargot in sauce veloute, broiled french-fried capon with sweet sauce, and lamprey in bearnaise. Quiche Dichondra is available for vegetarians. **Total cost of 12-meal package: $9,203.65.** (Just about what you'd pay to fly and eat, without the discomfort of actually having to get on board.)

#131301 MOUSIE TAILS Selected domestic coiled mouse tails, in exotic fruit sauce, delightful with ice cream, **$7.50 for 25 tails. Imported kangaroo mouse tails, $25.00.** Whole candied kangaroo: sorry, only on special order.

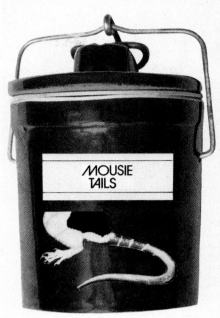

#121212 J. ISCARIOT LAST SUPPER Full pre-frozen supper for twelve (thaws in minutes in micro-wave) includes lamb, splendid fresco for dining-room decoration. Single rich chocolate kiss (guests vie to win it!). Special wines of fine transitional body available: Manischewitz-Mouton, Mogen-Montrachet. For the guest you especially wish to honor (big-wig at the office?) optional styrofoam cross, gilt crown of thorns: he'll know you went all out on his behalf! Later in evening, clever clockwork cock crows thrice.

Price: 30 pieces of silver.

Shipped from Gethsemane

#22522 PROFESSOR MITTELMITZER'S CHEESE-CAKE WHEEL Exact replica of heavy-duty stoneware wheel on which Professor Mittelmitzer (dynamic head of the Cheesecake Formation Institute at Aix-les-Fromages) threw the WORLD-PRIZE WINNING GRAND TRIANON REVERSIBLE CHEESECAKE in 1972! Holistic cheesecake kit leads you step by step from tiny hand-patted cakes to genuine architectural splendor! Foot-pedal or battery.

Price: $875.00. Supplies, equipment require continuous refrigeration.

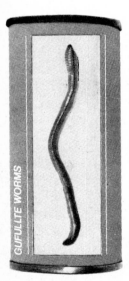

#655 KOSHER GOURMET DELICACY: GUFULLTE WORMS Six-foot Australian Earthworms, marinated in secret Kosher spicing sauce, bottled and shipped for your holiday enjoyment. Every step of the process supervised by Orthodox Rabbi.

Case of 6 1 lb. bottles: $165.00. Shipped from Sydney.

#633 HOME GROWN TRUFFLES Disturbed by the high price of French, Italian truffles? Menus upset? Our remarkable kit includes one oak tree, suitable soil, prepacked spores, and one simulated pig. Not guaranteed for regions with heavy winter frost.

F.O.B. Marseilles: $3500.00 includes recipe booklet, tree-planting suggestions.

#644 BREEZE DRIED MEAT High on Mount Tamalpais, full sides of beef, pork, penguin ripen and shrivel, then are sliced with old fashioned 2-man timber saws before being wrapped in dry Eucalyptus leaves and packed. NO additives, NO artificial ingredients. **Price varies,** depends on quotations at Chicago Board of Stock Futures.

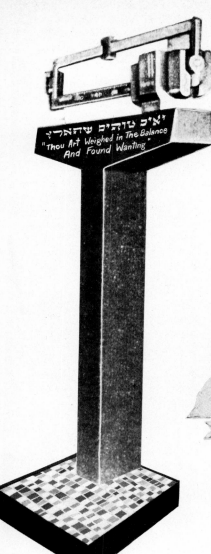

#4&20 MOTHER MACREEZE PIE MiX. Everything you need for an entire deep dish surprise: 4 & 20 Blackbirds (flash frozen) from the Bulgarian Forests, Puff Pastry, and seasonings. Completely ready for either oven or microwave facilities.

Total Cost: $4.20 per pie.

#730.00 BIBLICAL REDUCING SCALE Take pounds off your weight! Scale comes with four-color mosaic inlay of King Nebuchadnezzar, ornate Hebrew lettering MENE MENE TEKEL UPHARSIN, and English translation: "Thou Art Weighed In The Balance And Found Wanting."

Exclusive Import from Daniel Enterprises, Babylon: $730.00.

#44 . PERSONALIZED CEREAL Household of picky eaters? No longer! Just throw cereal into boiling water, and watch it automatically spell out names. Child eats name; ego-builder. Available in all letters except X, Z. **Dozen alphabets only $15.00. Boiling water not included.**

#131308 **SATELLITE DEBRIS** An international experience! Bits from American, Russian, Chinese, Israeli rockets and satellites, guaranteed to have flamed down through the stratosphere; surcharge for pieces that have inflicted wounds.

**Priced by weight: $1,000.00 per Kilo;
Bloody Kilo: $1,500.00.
Excitement! Delivery guaranteed through your own roof!**